OUT OF THE CRAZYWOODS

AMERICAN INDIAN LIVES
Series Editors

Kimberly Blaeser
University of Wisconsin, Milwaukee

Brenda J. Child
University of Minnesota

R. David Edmunds
University of Texas at Dallas

K. Tsianina Lomawaima
Arizona State University

Out of the Crazywoods

CHERYL SAVAGEAU

UNIVERSITY OF NEBRASKA PRESS   LINCOLN

Library of Congress Cataloging-in-Publication Data
Names: Savageau, Cheryl, 1950–, author.
Title: Out of the Crazywoods / Cheryl Savageau.
Description: Lincoln : University of Nebraska Press,
2020. | Series: American Indian lives | Includes
bibliographical references. | Summary: "Out of the
Crazywoods is the insightful and riveting story of
Abenaki poet Cheryl Savageau's late-life diagnosis of
manic depression (also known as bipolar disorder)
and her personal journey toward the acceptance
and management of this life-long illness to achieve
emotional stability"—Provided by publisher.
Identifiers: LCCN 2019035398
ISBN 9781496219039 (hardback)
ISBN 9781496220158 (epub)
ISBN 9781496220165 (mobi)
ISBN 9781496220172 (pdf)
Subjects: LCSH: Savageau, Cheryl, 1950– | Savageau,
Cheryl, 1950—Mental health. | Manic-depressive
illness—United States—Biography. | Women
authors, American—21st century—Biography.
Classification: LCC PS3569.A836 Z46
2020 | DDC 818/.5403 [B]—dc23
LC record available at
https://lccn.loc.gov/2019035398

Set in Alda by Mikala R. Kolander.
Designed by N. Putens.

for Chris

"... you weep night and day
to know that you were not abandoned,
that happiness saved its most extreme form
for you alone."

JANE KENYON

"The sadness will last forever."

VINCENT VAN GOGH

"... if my demons were to leave me, my angels may leave, too ..."

RAINER MARIA RILKE

CONTENTS

OUT OF THE CRAZYWOODS

it is what we call them
those places grown back
after the forest was cut down
crazywoods and we walk
crazy among them . . .

About This Book

Everything in this book was most likely written while I was in a hypo-manic state. Of course, because if I wasn't manic, I wouldn't be writing, I'd be sleeping, or staring at the shower curtain trying to remember why I should take a shower anyway, or staring at the unfinished paintings in my studio and thinking if I want to paint I'll have to clear the table, and get some water, and take my paints and brushes out of the tote bag I used when I went to class. But I'm writing, so there's mania there. But not so much that I'm thinking too fast for my fingers, or knitting twenty-seven hats, or flying around somewhere doing I don't know what the hell trying to get away from all those people walking around in slow motion just to fucking irritate me. And I'm not in one of those mixed states where all the shades are down, and I feel like shit, but I can't stand still, and I can't tell whether it's me trembling, or the car vibrating, and everything feels like an assault and I'm so fucking agitated you don't want to hear about it anyway. But you probably will.

Bagw and Tekw

We are studying language together. We've made flash cards with pictures on them and words on the reverse, so we can quiz each other. We will never be fluent, never really be able to speak. But it is something, this learning. Nebi, water. Nebizon, medicine water. Also, those streams of experience that flow through us and make up our own personal power. I am amazed. I wrote a whole poem to express this concept that is contained in one word in our language.

Tekw is moving. Bagw is stillness. River is tekw. Lake is bagw. Stream is tekw. Pond is bagw. Ocean is bagw. Waves are tekw.

All life is water, and water in a shifting balance, from tekw to bagw and back again. The trees know about water—their blood runs up the maple every spring carrying sugar stored from the year before, sustenance to grow the new leaves, and enough for us to share. The sap is tekw. The leaves are bagw. Wanabagwa.

You wouldn't think leaves and stillness, just looking at a tree, how the leaves move in the slightest breeze, how they rustle against each other in the wind. But a deeper look into the tree, into the movement within the tree, and you see the tree as part of the circle of water, and the leaves as places of stillness. The sap, the blood of the tree, runs in rivers up to the branches and twigs, then finds a resting place in the leaves, as brooks flow into a pond. The leaf is the place that holds water and sunshine and air for the great transformation to occur. Where water and carbon dioxide become sweet food and oxygen.

Bagw and tekw, stillness and movement. I want to learn from this. I want to find the calm stillness of a pond, and the clear flow of running water. We, like the trees who are our ancestors, are beings of water. My rivers run high, with rapids and whirlpools the stories say were created by the impetuous twin. The ponds have stagnated, become places with no give and take. The sunlight hurts, there is no sweetness here. Nothing flows in or out, no breeze moves the surface.

Under the Crib

I am under my crib with my ABC blocks and their little wagon with its red and white pulling rope. I tip the blocks over and the colors and lines change. I put one on top of the other. I throw them and watch them slide on the linoleum. I put them in the wagon, roll them back and forth, and take them back out again. I taste them, I bite them, I rub them on my face.

Now there is light streaming into the room. It is coming through the window, and there is dancing in the light. Something alive and magical is in the light. If only I could be in the light, could be the light, dance in the light. I am filled with love and awe and happiness.

But then the light dims, the dancing ones are gone. I am in shadow, alone under my crib. I look at my blocks. They are in shadow too. I don't want to play with them. I am waiting for the light to come back.

It is the artist's vision, this first memory. I bring up the memory at will, the magical dust motes dancing in the sun's rays, the numinous moment, the intake of breath, the widening of the eyes. The invitation. The mystery.

Then the shadow. The magic has turned dark, everything is grey. My cheek muscles go slack. I suck the inside of my lip.

The Pivot Point

It was the autumn before my mother died, the fall my nerves broke—do people still say that? It is how it feels. The September after the rabies shots, before my son's marriage, after my husband and I got back together, the year it seemed my whole life turned.

Maybe it was the doctor telling me I had high blood pressure two weeks after my fiftieth birthday and the move to Nashua; or maybe before that to the fall on the ice at the house on the pond and my drunk brother taking me to the ER; or maybe it began with the quilts I made in the dining room of the working-class Victorian in Nashua's North End, where you could see down to the cellar where the boards of the rough wood flooring didn't meet, where a thin dust blew up between the cracks, and wallpaper from the thirties faded on the cracking plaster.

The clock began ticking loudly the night my heartbeat changed. My heart jumped around my chest like popcorn in a popper. Maybe it was too much caffeine, or maybe it was that my husband was keeping things from me again, or maybe it was the moment my mother began to die.

I feel it now as a pivot point, the before and after, the moment when everything changed. If nerves are trees with intertwined branches, then those branches in me are lightning-struck, torn and broken.

Learning to Speak

My mother always told me that I sang before I could speak. Of course, she also told me that I was toilet trained at ten months. I think she was the one trained, not me, but I listen to her when she tells me about the singing.

This sense of music preceding speech has always intrigued me. What did I sing, Ma? Sure it would be a song still close to my heart, or maybe she meant I hummed some baby idea of melody. But no.

It was a song by Ray Charles, she says. And begins to sing to me. I am stunned. This was my first song? *Cry?* This song about heartache, about bad dreams and the blues? After all the trouble my mother went through to name me something that sounded like "cheerful," something she wished for me, even if it couldn't be pronounced in French. *Cry?*

You were speaking before you were a year, she says. A chatterbox by eighteen months. Even giving her leeway in terms of timing, I am stunned. How could I have latched on to this song as my first utterance? I try to hear my baby voice singing. I surprise myself by remembering all the words, though I have no memory of my infant self singing this. It is my mother's voice I hear. What part did I sing? What did my mother hear? And was this knowledge of the beautiful sadness of life something that I somehow already knew?

When my grandson first picked up a pencil, at just over a year, he held it correctly, as if he remembered from another life. Six months later, he'd forgotten how, grabbing the crayons in his fist like any two-year-old.

We have all been this way before. Who is this baby-self singing about heartache, and how did my mother stand it?

What It Is

They pretend to know. Sometimes you're up, sometimes you're down. Sometimes the blues just won't let go. The roller-coaster disease.

There are poles involved, like north and south, see this ice floe we're riding on? Watch out—the water's cold. You'll probably fall asleep. Bipolar. Can you say it? BiPolar Soda. The Penguin joins the Bear, we are all climbing the water tower together. If I said that in therapy it would be delusional. Out here on the ice floe it's just a joke.

There is something about transistors. The transistors in my brain are doing their own thing. How can I hear myself at night? The radio under my pillow, transistors working, Martha and the Vandellas singing *Love Is Like a Heat Wave*. Neurotransistors. Burning in my heart.

So these neurotransmitters are transmitting too much, or too little, and generally fucking with the chemistry of my brain. It's not that I'm see-sick, not Tigger at the top of the tree crying, *I see too much and I get sick*. Not like that at all.

Now it's about thermostats. Apparently, I don't have one. Funny, I always thought it was the laws of physics. *A body at rest tends to stay at rest; a body in motion tends to stay in motion.* I do that superbly.

But okay. If they want to talk about weather. It seems they all prefer warm, sunny days. A Southern California kind of day. I'm from the Northeast. I prefer WEATHER. Storms. A little rain on the pond. A three-day blizzard. Wind blowing leaves down sidewalks. I dream of tornadoes.

But they are saying too many days of rain demands an ark. And I can't hang glide forever, I could get lost, and eventually the wind will fail.

Okay. But what if I never again get to stand naked in the rain? What if I never get to be a human bird, soaring on the thermals?

That's the price you pay. The price for what? The price for what?

Age Three—The Witch in the Bag

It's Halloween. We are walking up the stairs to our apartment in Memere's house where we live with her. I'm carrying candy we bought for Trick-or-Treaters. I'm not too excited about going out in the dark, the cold air and scary people walking in the streets with white pillowcases and grocery bags. I know they are costumes, but I also know what I see: bones walking down the street, sheets billowing as the ghosts run to meet their friends, hair growing on people's knuckles.

Last year I went as a bunny, my mother said. I don't think the bunny will be safe outside. I remember when we got the kittens and they ran into the poison ivy and my father had to rescue them before the dogs got them. Everyone tells me I was so cute in the bunny costume, but when my mother takes it out it is dingy grey and I don't want to wear it.

My mother tells me how nice it is, and tries to make the floppy ears stand up a little straighter. My cousins wore this costume before I did and what might once have been pink is faded and sad. The white tail looks like a puppy chewed on it. This is not an Easter Bunny, or a Peter Rabbit Bunny, it is a Sad Bunny and I know I will be the Sad Bunny if my mother wants me to.

As Memere and I get to the top of the stairs, I see something in front of the door. It is a fancy shopping bag, with handles, the kind only my Gramma Delia uses when she goes to fancy stores. What's that? I ask. I am a little afraid to approach it. Open it and see, Memere says.

I look into the bag and see a tall, black pointy thing, and when I pull it out, Memere tells me it is a hat. A witch's hat. It is silky and shiny and a little scary. There's a shiny black dress and a ropey orange belt. There's a black mask and a funny broomstick, just my size. Witches ride on broomsticks, Memere says. They're magic.

Inside, I pull the dress over my head. I put on the mask, and then the hat, and Memere fixes the elastic under my chin so it doesn't snap. When I look in the mirror, it's not me. But it is me. A scary, witchy me. With a magic broomstick. I will be safe outside in the dark. I will be a witch forever.

Angels

Rob sees angels in the parking lot. He tries to tell us about them. They looked just like ordinary people, he says, but they were angels. His eyes are opened wide, he is awestruck. The sun comes in the open window behind him, his dark hair glows with a gold aura. He drops his backpack from his shoulders. The world is full of angels, he says, trying to get through to us, grabbing our eyes with his. He knows they are angels, he says, because he can see their goodness.

I want to see goodness in people in the parking lot. Does that make me crazy? Is he crazy to see this? Or is he childlike? Christlike? Does he have the Buddha-light? Is it all a matter of how you say it?

Here is what they say about Rob. They say he is delusional. They say he is bipolar this year, last year schizophrenic, next year who knows. They say he doesn't want to take his meds. They say he is noncompliant. They say he is difficult to be around. They say you never know what he is going to say. They say what he says is unsettling, you might not want to hear it. They say he can't take care of himself, that sometimes he forgets to bathe, forgets to eat. Sometimes he drops out of sight and we don't see him for weeks.

Rob wants to tell us everything. He is not background music, he is jazz, you have to pay attention.

Rob is not the Dalai Lama, not a prophet. He is just Rob, who sees things other people don't see. Like angels. In the parking lot.

Diagnosis

The diagnosis came late for me. Classic bipolar. The shrink has done what no one else has ever done. He's taken a life history. I am not simply a depressive with an anxiety disorder. Those flights of creativity, those numinous insights, those trips to the bookstore when I find twenty-seven books that are all somehow mystically related to each other, those weeks when I stay up until 4 a.m. writing, playing piano, making quilts. Those don't happen to depressives. They happen to people with bipolar.

I know he is mistaken. Bipolar. Manic Depression. That's really crazy. Not respectably depressed, garden variety, everyone's-on-the-latest-SSRI-it's-nothing-to-worry-about depression. Except I can't get out of bed, or if I get out of bed I can't shower—it's just too much work. And if I do get up and eat breakfast, I fall asleep afterwards. If I even think about going into the studio, I just look at everything. It is too much effort to get water for painting or to sit down at the sewing machine. If I put a couple of swatches on the design wall, they don't move me at all. I just walk away.

But there are those days I wake up, go into my studio, talk a blue-streak to my friends at lunch, work night after night. I barely need to sleep at all. My aches and pains are mysteriously gone.

I write forty poems in three weeks. I make five quilts in two months. I knit a huge hat and put it in the washing machine to felt it. It's so cool I go to the yarn store and buy hundreds of dollars of yarn, and make two dozen more. This could be a business. I spend afternoons figuring out the amounts of each kind of yarn I would need for each hat.

Then I am sick of yarn. I put it away. I will make hats again, I tell myself, but six years later, the yarn is still in the cedar chest. I don't make hats anymore, now I'm into gourds. I tell myself, Picasso had his blue period, his pink, his cubism. So I have my quilt period, my hat period, my gourd period.

He is medicalizing the artistic temperament, I tell my friends. I am not bipolar. I am not manic-depressive. I've never driven to a casino in the middle of the night and gambled away our money. I've never fucked the football team or the girls softball team, though I might have wanted to. Give me a little artistic license, for Chrissakes. So I'm not "normal," whatever the fuck that is. I'm an artist. These things happen.

Dirt

This is the year when everything becomes possible. I spend most of every day in the sand piles. The houses I build are domes, and I want to live in them. I find little twigs and plant them around every house. I don't make roads, just paths, winding their way between the round houses. I make houses with my hands, and with popsicle sticks I've picked up and saved from under the bleachers at the little league field down the road. I make houses with my hands because trucks and bulldozers are for boys.

When the sand pile is full of houses, I go into the back yard. We've just moved to this house my parents have built. My grandmother moved with us. The backyard is a vastness of deep grooves from the heavy equipment. They are deep trenches I can walk in. The sides reach to my chest in some places. My father says they will plant grass back here, but for now it's all dark brown dirt, the best for making mud. I make mud pies and stack them on every layer of the wall my father made out of cement blocks. My grandmother bakes, my mother bakes. I will be a baker.

One day, when I fall and get dirt in my mouth, my grandmother tells me not to cry. You'll eat a peck of dirt before you die, she says. I think it is a rule. That before you can die you have to eat a peck of dirt. What if you don't? I ask her. What if you haven't eaten a whole peck? It seems impossible to me. Don't worry, you will, she says.

But I'm not so sure. There is sand in my mouth and tiny stones. What if you haven't? Will someone force you to eat all that dirt at once? I know how big a peck is. We buy pecks of potatoes. That's a lot of dirt. Just to make sure, every time I make a mud pie, I stick my tongue out and just . . . touch it. That way, I figure, I'll definitely have eaten my peck of dirt long before my time to die. No one's gonna make me eat it all at once.

She's Not Heavy, She's My Sister

When I call my sister to tell her about the diagnosis, she must hear in my voice how scared and frustrated I am. What do you think? I ask.

You have to think about your life, and whether what they are telling you makes sense, she says.

Yes, but what do you think? Do you think he's right?

Well, I don't know, Cher, but I do know whenever we talk you're either really enthusiastic about some new thing you're into, or you're in the middle of a crisis.

Yeah, I say. I guess that's true.

What she didn't say was, Cher, I'm terrified. She told me this later—how all of a sudden she had a sibling with a major mental illness.

But I wasn't thinking of her. Not then. I was thinking about me. Was I bipolar? I'd told the doctor, no, I am not bipolar, you're wrong. But now, on the phone with my sister, I'm not so sure. I'm hoping she, who has known me longest of anyone, will see the truth. Am I crazy? Am I sick?

At a family party, I'm sitting next to my cousin, Nadine, five years younger than me. She was diagnosed with bipolar twenty years ago. Her brother is talking about Alzheimer's. It must be awful, he says, losing your mind like that. I give Nadine a nudge and say, we don't have to worry about that, we've already lost ours. We start giggling like kids in church, unable to stop ourselves.

She has had a terrible time with medications. Her hands tremble all the time. Everyone treats her as if she is incompetent, fragile. When we leave the room to get something to eat, she speaks in a confident voice, but when we return to the sunroom to sit with our families, she is tentative in everything she does, everything she says, waiting to be corrected or criticized. Everything she does is a symptom. Will they treat me like that now, too?

My sister wants to help, but she doesn't know how. She and I have always been oil and water. We love each other, but fall into decades of family roles and patterns. In spite of my science background, I am the artist, she is the scientist. She is practical, I am, well . . . not.

I give her a book on bipolar, one I've found particularly helpful. I want to discuss it with her, but she says she's read it and knows all about bipolar disorder. I am stunned by what she says, because I don't know all about it. I am lost in the crazywoods, and she can't follow the trail to find me. It is too scary to be in these woods. She wants to get in and get out as fast as we can. But there is no quick route out. Only picking through these overgrown paths.

She is scared and frustrated and angry. When I go to live with her, I stay inside most of the time, read, watch TV, play on the computer, write in my journal.

Why don't you take a walk, she scolds me. You can't just sit around like that. What are you going to be like at seventy if you can barely get around now? I can hear her disapproval, but not her worry. I am defective, the way I always feel around family.

She wants to help me, but she doesn't know how. Neither of us does. She hasn't seen me when I can't get out of bed, can't shower or wash my hair. She doesn't know that just getting those things done is a victory. And I can't tell her. I can't will myself out of this depression.

The Tarot

There are over twenty decks in the maple chest. The Rider Waite deck is the first deck I owned, the learning deck, the Mother of all twentieth century decks. The second deck, the round Motherpeace deck with its childlike and women-centered images, is the feminist deck. I am the woman bathing in moonlight.

There's the New World Tarot, with wood carvings painted in jewel colors, and the Morgan Greer, one of my favorite reading decks, the one I go to for unadorned answers. The Fey Tarot, with powerful Fairies you've never imagined, the quiet Hudes deck, and the Tarot of Prague, where the first golem was made and, some say, still sleeps.

There is the Fairytale Tarot, which makes me smile, but tells the truth, and the Animal Lords who have the bodies of humans, the heads of beasts. The Goddess Tarot is luminous, each card a Goddess-Yemanji, Kwan Yin-I become them all. And the Buddha Tarot where I build meditations and visit four mountains.

I have spent a lot of time choosing the right homes for these decks. Some are wrapped in silk scarves. Some are in embroidered and beaded bags. One deck is in a round black box, painted with lilies. A few are still in their original boxes, waiting.

These are the journeys I take now, far from the witchcraft in the outside world, journeys through the cards, through dimensions where the figures in the cards talk to me, tempt me to stay longer than I should, give me gifts. I remember that when in the land of Faerie, you mustn't eat or drink or you may be caught there, an evening twenty years, a lifetime in an afternoon. I spend entire days lost in the cards, laying out one spread after another, changing decks and comparing results, and time passes without my knowing.

I am trying to find my life in these cards.

In this card, the young man sits cross-legged on the lotus flower and plays flute for me. I breathe the music in like incense. The tall woman in purple looms over me. I look up into her distant face, but she does not speak. I join the three women dancing, dancing. We are sisters, we are young, we are dancing, holding hands in the sun, in the moonlight.

Beware the swords, they are all sorrow. Here is the one I fear, the night-mare card. It is the Bosch painting over the lovers' bed. The heart pierced three times.

A woman is walking toward me across a plain of swaying grass, her hand in the mane of a lion. She is all red and gold fire. She knows I want her.

I spread the cards in crosses, in rows, circles, and pyramids. I am riding on the rim of a giant wheel—where it stops nobody knows.

The dog is barking at the top of the stairs, the woman is floating out of her body, the man is hanging by one foot.

I am the woman dancing drunk on the roof, too close to the edge.

Tiger Butter

Our bathroom was not a big one. There was the narrow space in front of the sink with its big round mirror borrowed from a bedroom dresser. There was a built-in medicine chest in the corner that held Band-Aids and Mercurochrome, and some weird gadget for earaches that I wasn't allowed to play with. The toilet was on the right, at the end of the room, across from the tub, which had a bluish curtain that was often left open so people could sit on the edge while waiting their turn.

There was a small window at the end of the room, and my father had managed to fit a bookcase under it that was a fixture throughout my childhood and until after his death, when I was in my thirties. In fact, the disappearance of the bookcase signaled to me that my father was really gone, that my mother was making the house her own, moving my father's things out.

My mother had never liked the bookcase in the bathroom, but she tolerated it and tried to keep it neat. It was filled with books we were reading, or had read, or would read. An ever-changing library for all ages. There were the All About books—a series of science books that came from a book club my mother, ironically, enrolled me in as a Christmas present in third grade. Every month a book came—*All About Birds, All About Volcanoes, All About Dinosaurs, All About the Atom, All About Mammals, All About Amphibians*—a couple of dozen in all, and all my siblings got their turns reading them.

My dad had mystery magazines, including Alfred Hitchcock's, whose stories I read along with Poe, Stevenson, Daphne du Maurier, Louisa

May Alcott, and Hawthorne. Shakespeare's sonnets that I felt rather than understood, and Eliot's "Preludes," where I discovered a poetry with everyday images from the poet known for his obscure references. Bradbury, Sturgeon, Asimov. *Jane Eyre*, which I read at least once a year. *Myths of the World. Grimm's Fairy Tales.* Biographies of Einstein, Beethoven, Madame Curie, and Jim Thorpe. *The Brothers Karamazov, Alice in Wonderland. How to Play Bridge.*

All of this and more moved through the bathroom library. From the *Conquests of Tamerlaine* I learned the euphemism "his throbbing manhood," and from *Catch-22,* the word "prophylactic," which the dictionary was vague about, and my father said was something that prevented disease the way brushing your teeth prevented cavities. And of course the Little Golden Books, the ones we all started with.

The Little Golden Books were the ones that my mother read to me while I sat on the toilet, she on the edge of the tub, holding the book so I could see the pictures. One book is *Little Black Sambo*—a book rightly vilified for its racism until the story was rescued years later by Julius Lester. My mother is reading, and I am crying.

The story began as many stories do, a Mother, a Father, a Child. I am four years old, and like the child in the story, I have no sisters or brothers yet. The child goes out into the woods, not like our woods, but jungle woods with palm trees and vines, and yes, Tigers.

The Tigers chase Sambo. I am not afraid for him. Sambo is quick and safe in the tree he's climbed, and the Tigers, the beautiful Tigers, run round and round the tree. Sambo and I look down at the Tigers running around the tree. They run so fast they almost catch each other's tails. They are a blur of orange, white, and black, and big yellow Tiger eyes. They run and run until they turn into butter.

At this point, I cry. Tears run into my mouth and down my chin. I cannot be comforted. The poor, beautiful Tigers. Even now it makes me want to cry. How could all that beauty and grace and terrifying strength become the crazy, but still beautiful, Tiger whirlwind that *turned them into butter?!!*

It was no comfort to me that Sambo collected the butter and brought it home. No comfort that it tasted so good on the pancakes his mother made. No comfort that his parents were proud of him.

Every day I asked for the story. Every day I cried. "What book do you want today?" my mother asked. "*Little Black Sambo*," I'd say. "That book always makes you cry. Wouldn't you like a different book?" But I was adamant. "*Little Black Sambo*," I insisted. And so she read the story, and I sobbed my grief. It was the fierce beauty of the Tigers, the circle of yellow around the tree, the mandala of Tigers spinning, spinning, intoxicating, magical, and then their sad demise, that drew me in.

I wanted the Tigers to stop running around the tree, for Sambo just to go home, and they back into the dark of the forest. But at the same time I was mesmerized. It was the heart of the story—the confrontation with mystery, the tragic, with passion, art, and the power of transformation.

I think I could love Tiger butter now, even though I am still filled with grief when I retell or recall the story. But with so much I counted on in my life now ripped away, with the Tigers chasing me, the whirlwind overwhelming me, I would welcome some Tiger butter that I could spread over good bread and savor and be saved.

LOOK

It's the first day of first grade and I'm at school wearing a blue plaid dress with a white collar and white and brown saddlebacks. The schoolroom has wood floors that are different from ours because they are ripply, they go up and down in little hills under my feet. There are silver radiators against the wall. I have never seen anything like them before. Windows rise above them up and up to the very high ceiling. It smells like paper and chalk.

There are pictures from nursery rhymes on the wall and the teacher asks us if we know what they are. We have to raise our hands. Everyone knows Jack Be Nimble Jack Be Quick, and Jack and Jill Went Up the Hill, and Little Miss Muppet Sat on a Tuffet. Nobody knows the one she's pointing to with a blond boy in a blue sailor suit. But I do. I raise my hand and she calls on me. I stand up and sing *Bobby Shafto went to sea, silver buckles on his knee, He'll come back and marry me, pretty Bobbie Shafto.* I'm used to performing—everyone sings at my house—I'm not shy about it, so when the teacher smiles and nods, I sing the second verse, too.

Then she says it's time to read. She has an easel at the front of the room and on it is a huge book, bigger than any book I've ever seen. I already know how to read, and I have been sneaking looks at it all day. Now I'm holding my breath. I want to see inside this mysterious book. The teacher sits next to the easel and opens to the first page. On it there is just one word: LOOK. I know it is the beginning of magic.

Age Seven—The Body Book

For Christmas my mother gives me a book. It's full of beautiful bones and muscles and blood cells. Everyone with their skin peeled back so you can look. Inside there are organs, and you can see how they are all connected. Mouth to stomach to intestines to colon, a long tunnel of transformation. Mouth to throat to bronchial tubes to lungs to blood to heart to everywhere in the whole body, and back again. The circle of breath. The brain with all its nerves like the branches on a maple tree. The kidneys like beans. The bones inside our ears and covering our knees. The tympanum. The patella.

Almost at the end, there are pictures of a baby growing inside its mother. It starts with a tiny cell and ends up a person. The baby, curled up like a seashell, the shape of the mother's womb—the body is all curves and secrets, and I am in love.

Poppies

Poppies, poppies will make them sleep . . .

In third grade, after many bouts with strep throat, I go to the hospital to have my tonsils out. But I don't get my tonsils out. When the doctor listens to my chest, he shakes his head and speaks to my parents at the end of the bed. My father comes over and tells me I'll have to come back another time. I can't have my tonsils out because I have a chest cold. But it isn't a chest cold. It's pneumonia. I heard them say it, and I know how to spell it.

I watch the other kids go upstairs, one after the other—there are six of us in this room—and come back with their hair plastered against their heads, their skin pale, eyes shut. When they wake up, they spit up blood into plastic trays. They can't cry, but they whine. I am scared for them and scared by them. The next morning they are all up eating jello and ice cream. They are happy and going home. I am not.

When I leave the hospital a few days later, I can't go to school. It's November, and I have to keep away from the front door because of the cold that rushes in when someone opens it, but I catch glimpses of early snow and night sky when my father comes home from work.

One night my father gets a call. My grandfather has died. This is the first time I've heard my father cry. I have never heard anyone cry like that before, in great gulping sobs. My grandfather died from a blood clot in his lung. Pneumonia is in my lungs. He was in the hospital like me, and now he's dead.

I am running through the field of poppies with Dorothy and the Scarecrow. The Lion is thumping along beside us, the Tin Man is clanging. We are running toward Emerald City, but I can't run. My legs are heavy, I need to run away. Now something is chasing us. Run. Run. But I can't run. I can't breathe, I can't breathe, I say. And then the voice says, "Of course you can't breathe. You're dead."

This is the dream I have over and over. For years, into adulthood. But this first night I have the dream, I wake up to a strange smell. I still can't breathe. I walk down the hall. I hear my parents talking. My mother is sitting on the cellar stairs. My father is finishing up painting the cellar floor. The smell is heavy around us as I climb slowly down the steps. My mother reaches out to me and I crawl into her lap.

Mama, am I dead?

What do you mean, are you dead? Of course you're not dead.

But I'm not breathing.

She tells me that of course I'm breathing. She makes me blow on my fingers. See, you couldn't do that if you were dead.

I'm afraid to go back to bed. I tell her about the dream. She comes back upstairs with me, climbs into bed beside me, and I am wrapped in her arms and warm body. I can hear my heart beating fast in my ears, and hers, beating steady and slow.

trees grow
every which way
in the crazywoods
undergrowth is thick
and sometimes
stops all progress

At the Welfare Office

The Department of Transitional Assistance is what they call it now. It is for emergency funds, they say. My caseworker says I'll get $300 plus food stamps per month. I am so relieved. At last I will have some money coming in, no matter how little.

I am living with my son Chris and his wife Marci, and my two grandchildren, ages eight and five. I haven't been able to contribute anything, even to groceries. At least with food stamps, I will be able to do that.

So I wait with my caseworker in line, get a form to fill out, then sit on a rickety chair with all the others in this room sitting on rickety chairs, waiting. I don't have the resigned face yet of the people around me. I am ignorant. I have the middle-class expectation that there is a procedure, that if I do what I am supposed to do, I will get what I'm supposed to, and go home. I don't know anything yet.

My hands are trembling. The waiting room is hot and tired and smells of lots of bodies, washed and not. There is a low buzz of people talking, but the place is actually surprisingly quiet. A baby starts crying, then another cries as if crying shouldn't be done alone, as if it's contagious. Maybe that's why everyone sits with shoulders down, eyes averted. If feelings spilled out we would have a riot or a wailing that would shake the building and alert the police. Although they need to hear us, the people in Washington would never know there was a meltdown in Brockton, Massachusetts, today. I wonder if I am the only one thinking this.

Finally it's my turn. The woman who can give me money says I can't get it today, I have to go to Social Security and get papers from them first. I look up at my caseworker, confused, and walk out of the office with her, shaking. Don't worry, she says. Do you feel well enough to go to Social Security? I nod my head, yes. I follow her as we walk into another waiting room. Finally we get the paper, and I can go home. I'll pick you up tomorrow, my caseworker says. I mumble okay, shut the door, and go to bed.

In the morning I know it's going to be another bad day. I am on edge. I am not holding it together. I'm waiting in DTA again and it's hard for me to sit still. This time I have a paper saying I applied at the Social Security Office. Now they should be able to give me the $150 they said I'd get, not the $300 my caseworker originally told me, and some food stamps.

But No. Now they want more. Now they want medical proof that I am disabled. I just gave all that to SSI. Why aren't their computers talking to each other, I want to know. No, they tell me, we are not connected to their system. We are totally separate.

I begin to lose it. I've been destitute since January, I tell them, staying with friends and family, essentially homeless, and now it's August, and you still can't help me. My voice is getting louder. What the hell does Emergency mean to this office? They try to shush me. Don't fucking tell me to be quiet, I say. What the fuck do you guys need to understand? I'm living a fucking emergency.

Don't use that language with me, the money woman says, calm down.

What the fuck do you mean, calm down? I can't work, I have no money, and you want more paperwork because your fucking computers aren't talking to each other? Now I'm into a full rant, I can feel my eyes widen, my nostrils flare.

Another woman is talking to me now, saying calm down, calm down, my caseworker is explaining that I'm bipolar, and I am saying it has fucking nothing do with being bipolar, I'm just fucking pissed that they're jerking me around when all I need is a little help through the next few months. I look at the woman who told me to calm down. Is it your fucking money? I'm still yelling as my caseworker guides me out of the office.

We'll get the paperwork together, don't worry about it, she is saying. I am still boiling, my thermostat hasn't kicked in. I have a right to be angry, it's true. But it's also true that my illness has taken over, I am out of control. My hands are shaking. I'm trembling all over. My caseworker is asking me if I'm all right, saying we'll get it done, don't worry.

I sit at the kitchen table at my son's house, where I am living for now, sobbing. This is how my daughter-in-law finds me.

What's the matter, what's happened, she asks me, and I tell her.

I'm out of control, I say. I think I need to be in the hospital. I need to be locked up somewhere. I'm dangerous. I'm crazy.

I don't realize how much I've frightened her. She meets my son in the driveway when he comes home and tells him I want to be committed. She doesn't need to be committed, he says. He's used to my breakdowns. Take the kids for a walk, he tells her.

He finds me at the kitchen table, sits in the chair across from me. What's up? he asks.

I'm crazy, I say. I can't cope. I need to be in the hospital.

No you don't, he says. Are you hungry?

He takes me to the diner, where he talks me down. This is just one bad day, he says. Think about how much you've accomplished this week. He lists my going to the Social Security office, twice, getting my license, going for a walk every day. Tomorrow will be better, he says.

I eat my grilled cheese, he eats a pastrami sandwich. You always know how to talk me down, I say. He nods. I'm sorry it's you who has to do that. Me too, he says. Comes with the territory.

It's several months before I can think about the welfare office without feeling ashamed. I don't want to be the crazy lady. I vow this will never happen again. I am more than the crazy lady. She will not run my life.

Exuberance

My sister and cousin are watching as Lucy and Ethel work on the candy assembly line. It starts off fine, but you know it's heading for disaster. I'm standing at the back of the living room, several feet behind them, watching it all unfold. The candy starts to move faster—Lucy and Ethel can't put the candy into the boxes, they are eating it, shoving it in, Lucy crawls onto the moving belt. It's chaos.

My sister and cousin are rolling on the floor, giggling. It's the Cecile and Doris show, they say. They see my mother and aunt behind the masks of Lucy and Ethel, the same as I do, but they are younger siblings, they think it's funny. All I can think is, who's going to fix this?

In the families of most people with bipolar disorder are those people who are always exuberant, with so much energy they make other people tired. My mother cycled between exuberance and anger. She didn't have depressive days when she stayed in bed.

She and my grandmother had set days for certain chores, as most people did back then. Monday laundry, Tuesday ironing, I don't know what on Wednesday and Thursday. Friday was wax-the-floor day.

My mother used bowling alley wax on the hardwood floors. She scooped the thick wax out of the gallon-size can, and loaded the brushes, pressing down with an old soup spoon to put in as much as possible. Then she waxed the floors of our five-room ranch that she and my father built, the living room, the hallway, the bedrooms, the kitchen and bathroom tiles. She was strong, my mother, and pushed the buffer around with enthusiasm.

But that was only stage one. The floors would be hazy and sluggish with dried wax, and we weren't supposed to go on them because we'd pull it off or leave lint from our socks. My mother turned the buffer upside down, pulled off the wax brushes, and slapped on the buffing brushes. Again, she'd walk the house, throwing the buffer out on its long leash and pulling it back over all the floors, singing, shining the beautiful wood. During the week, she did touch-ups with the buffer, but the wax was only applied on Friday.

That included Good Friday, the day that Jesus died. We were supposed to be silent all afternoon. I could do that easily if I had a book to read. But we weren't supposed to be enjoying ourselves, we were supposed to be thinking about our sins, and Jesus dying on the cross.

One Good Friday when I was maybe nine years old, we were walking around almost on tiptoes. My friend Terry and I had worked out an elaborate sign language that we'd convinced ourselves was not really talking. We had several secret languages, including one that consisted solely of blocking our sinuses so we sounded like we had bad colds. This was our first try at sign language, and it wasn't working all that well. Especially after my mother realized what we were doing and sent Terry home, using her own sign language that included opening the front door and pointing Terry toward her house.

I was resigned to silence. The only ones talking were my baby brothers, one only three, one not walking yet, but burbling in his baby language. My grandmother picked him up from time to time and tried to get him to sleep, but he just grabbed at her face, exploring her lips and nose. I curled up on the sofa with a school book, boring enough to be acceptable. My sister practiced touching her toes to her head, her back arching as she lay on her belly on the hooked rug we were all working to finish. My three-year-old brother ran his truck back and forth, back and forth, then laid his head on the dog's belly and fell asleep.

My mother was busy in the kitchen. We could hear her moving around, dragging something, clattering sounds, and then the whine of the buffer. It was Friday, she would buff the floors. Sunday was Easter. How could the floors not be at their best? My sister and I both headed for the kitchen, where Ma was buffing beneath the table, upon which she'd upended all the chairs. We looked on in disbelief. Was buffing not included in the silence rule?

Up and down the hall, into every bedroom, and finally over the expanse of the living room floor, my mother ran the buffer through its full routine, the applying of wax, the buffing and shining. Through the whole afternoon the machine whined, my baby brother cried from the loud noise, while my sister, my grandmother, and I were silent. My mother never spoke a word. As far as she was concerned, she had kept the silence.

My mother never seemed tired after buffing, or any other strenuous activity—she had an athlete's endurance. She'd heat up the teakettle and sit with a cup before zooming into activity again. She had a sweet tooth, and made desserts every day, devil's food cake with chocolate frosting made in a long pan, so she could cut them into squares for servings and lunches—each square with its own walnut; date squares with white frosting and coconut flakes. Tomato soup cake with cream cheese frosting, my father's favorite. Brownies. Cookies. Pies.

My mother made pies so often that my grandmother found a special triangle-shaped plastic tub so I could carry slices of pie to school. I never knew what my mother might be baking when I got home. Baklava, which she learned from my best friend Terry's mother, who was Lebanese. At holidays she might be making angel wings, with dough twisted through itself, deep-fried and dipped in powdered sugar, or pixelles, which were made from a batter into which you dipped metal snowflakes on the end of long metal arms, and deep-fried, also covered with confectioner's sugar. She was always in the middle of a whirlwind—this one, the sweet baking whirlwind.

My mother's enthusiasm extended to shopping—which was always a challenge. We shopped at the Mart, The Fair, Bradlees, and at Spag's, the overgrown general store that had twists and turns, a ramp that led to what had been a separate building, goods piled so high it was like walking through a maze. The clothes didn't last long, the elastic in the underwear gave out, the socks grew holes. Which was either a curse or a blessing, depending on whether or not you liked shopping.

When I was a freshman in high school, my mother had entered a religious phase—she was taking classes at Assumption College about Old Testament Prophecies, about Morals, about Mary and her mother, St. Anne. My mother had always been pious, but in a personal way. Now these classes fed an intellectual need that might have blossomed in a college education she never had. But then, there is that tendency in the family to have this religious fervor at certain times in our lives.

My aunt Anita, the musician, went from Catholicism to the Baptists, to what my grandmother called the Holy Rollers, and back to the Catholic Ecstatics. She was an alcoholic, and religion was her second drug. She was slain in the spirit. She talked in tongues. She shook and praised and was filled with the Holy Spirit. She met a lot of people who needed a place to stay who would end up living at her house, getting drunk every night, and singing while she played piano. My cousins said there was a whole lot of shaking going on, and it wasn't all about the Holy Spirit.

In the midst of her religious kick, my mother decided we all needed to go to Catholic schools. My parents had worked as youth advisors with the young handsome priest at our church, and had become friends. When the diocese moved him to a new parish with its own elementary and high schools, my mother decided it was the place for us to go.

When my mother made this decision I loved the public school I was in. I was in an honors class, and for the first time I had friends who read books. We talked for hours on the phone after school—about Marx, Huxley, Darwin. Holden Caulfield and Yossarian, 1945 and 1984.

If you make me take the test, I'll flunk it, I told them when my parents signed me up to take the test to get into St. Peter's. I'll know the answers, so I can just put the wrong ones instead of the right ones. Just take the test, my mother said, no one's saying you have to go. So I took the test, trusting them, and besides, it's really hard to put the wrong answer when you know the right one. Tests were like being on *Jeopardy*. Filling in all those little circles with my number two pencil gave me the same rush as saying the answers at home before the *Jeopardy* contestants.

So it was partly my fault that in the fall, despite my mother's promise, I found myself a freshman at St. Peter's Central Catholic High School. The school was in a rough section of Worcester, the city across the lake from where we lived. I'd only ever been in the city when we took the bus downtown to the movies. My friends and I browsed Woolworth's and Newbury's, bought a slice of pizza at the take-out, and walked through the common. We never left that block around City Hall. But this was real city with run-down three-deckers, a boarding house across the street, a few short blocks from the train tracks and gas tanks. I took up smoking and swearing, and learned to look tough. I checked myself out in the mirror each morning, put on my tough face, tossed my hair.

There were no science labs. There was no caf, so we ate in the basement sitting on the benches between rows of lockers. The teachers were all teaching outside their fields, for the discipline, so we had a Latin teacher teaching us science, an English teacher teaching us math, and a math teacher teaching history. I got in trouble for questioning the Adam-and-Eve story, when I pointed out that snakes have no vocal cords, for pointing out mistakes in our seriously out-of-date science book, and for smoking in the girls' room, part of my looking-tough strategy.

My sister and brother were going to the grammar school next door, and my mother picked them up at three o'clock. Or that was the plan. A couple of my friends and I had taken to stopping at the Greek's, a diner on the corner, after school, then taking the bus downtown to transfer home. But that didn't last long.

My mother and aunt had discovered thrift stores. The racks and racks of bargains, dresses, coats, blouses, pants, shoes, and hats. They started to be late picking up my brother and sister. My sister told me my brother cried because he was scared. It was starting to be a Lucy-and-Ethel misadventure.

So I stopped going downtown, had my Coke at the corner, then waited with my sister and brother for my mother to come. Lucy would arrive with Ethel in tow, laughing, having had a great time, and wanting to include us in her mirth, as if she wasn't fifteen, twenty, forty-five minutes late. As if this wasn't a dangerous part of town. Why would they worry? I was there to keep everybody safe.

My mother was always full of stories of their adventures and all the great bargains they'd found. I wasn't that late, was I? she'd say. And then laugh, all flirty eyes, inviting us in to share her wonderful enthusiasm. Except I couldn't. I wasn't Lucy. I wasn't even Ethel. I was just me, making sure nothing bad happened.

My sister doesn't understand why I can't laugh at Lucy, although now I can laugh at my mother buffing the floors in the midst of imposed silence. I think it is as silent as she could be. My mother was the fun mother, unpredictable, playful, always having another idea. Let's play Bingo, have a parade, fly kites, make blueberry pies. My sister and my little brothers were always ready for whatever my mother dreamed up. I was skeptical of all her enthusiasms. When would they turn into trouble? When would the assembly line break down and the candies go spilling onto the floor?

Shopping

I love to go shopping. I hate to go shopping. I'm so glad there is a word to describe this. Ambivalent. I am ambivalent about shopping. I have a love/hate relationship with shopping. In the bookstore, I pick up a book, open randomly to a page, and read from a poem by Kabir:

> Inside this clay jug
> are canyons and pine mountains
> and the maker of canyons and pine mountains
> and hundreds of millions of stars

Inside these twenty-seven books are hundreds of millions of stars . . . oh, yes, I know about this, I need this book. And this one about Celtic women, and this cookbook, and these novels, and this history of small-pox. They are all magically connected. I don't know how yet, but I can feel it. Twenty-seven books, full of encounters with the mysterious. My arms are full, my hope is in my arms, the breaking of all boundaries, unbounded love. I am enveloped by the numinous, and how I love that word—numinous, luminous, yes, it is both. I am happy at the register as the woman listens to me telling her about these wondrous books, as I slip my card through the machine, as I put in the magic twenty-sevens.

At home, I am busy on the computer, buying Tarot cards. I have sixteen decks by now, and I love them all. I am choosing more, and I choose carefully. They have to embody the mystery. And there are so many ways to do this. Each deck expands upon the next. I take out the cards and look at all the renditions of the Hermit card, how he is either coming or going, how she is on a mountain, or a road, how the colors are blue or lavender, lighted or dark. It all comes together in a spectrum that makes up the reality of the archetype, like a sacred jigsaw puzzle. Soon I will have twenty-seven decks.

You have to understand that when I say twenty-seven, I don't really mean twenty-seven. It's just a figure of speech, like "it rained for forty days and forty nights," or "forty days in the desert," or "three's the charm," or in this case three times three times three. Three to the third power. Twenty-Seven. I like the feel of it my mouth. This is a gift. As a poet I can use this. I teach my students, Learn what words feel good in your mouth. I don't tell them about my twenty-sevens. I'm not obsessive-compulsive, I don't walk around my desk twenty-seven times or anything. It's just a figure of speech.

I'm shopping for coats today. It was supposed to snow this morning, but it didn't, but it will soon, so I should have a coat. The one from last winter doesn't zip right and I hate it anyway, and I've had it for five years—it's time for a new coat. I'm not worried on the way to the store. I'm going to Burlington Coat Factory, and my therapist told me there's lots of sizes there. So I'm cool.

I turn the music up loud and sing along so I won't have to think. I can just lose myself in the sound. My son said one time when he was a boy, I don't know why I sound so much better when I sing with the record than by myself. I am laughing while I sing, because he is so right. I can reach every note Joni Mitchell is singing. I love her, I think we'll play that one again. Why didn't I become a singer?

So this is the problem. I find three coats that fit. One is a black short coat with a hood and fake fur. The other is a long wool coat, also with fake fur. Fake fur is apparently very in this year. But these coats are both great. Then I find a beautiful brown suede coat, with brown fur. I try them all on. They all look good. I can't decide. I enlist the help of fellow shoppers. Eventually one of them has to go back to work, but she says she had fun shopping with me.

I still can't decide. I don't have a dressy coat, so I really should get the long coat, but then I can't wear it every day, and what if I want to go for a walk in the woods? The short black coat fits me great, and it's classic, the girl said who was helping me, and the hood is detachable, and it's waterproof. But it's a lot like the one I'm going to throw out, only not really because that one is that shiny material and this is matte, and last year's coat had that stupid zipper and this one has buttons. I pull my hair out of the collar and the white/silver looks cool against the black and matches the rims of my glasses.

I try the brown one on again. I love suede and this is a country jacket for the woods, I would blend into the trees and Abenaki are relatives to the trees. But now that I have white hair I shouldn't wear brown, my daughter-in-law says. So I try the other coats on again. I still can't decide. One more time. The long coat, the short coat, the brown suede. Dammit. I give up in despair and walk out of the store. Or else, I buy all three.

Crazy Lady in Grad School

She was a grad student, a doctoral candidate. But her presence was intimidating. She was a big woman, tall, heavy, with long, wild, light brown hair in disheveled curls, all kind of ratty.

Her clothes were equally wild. I remember more an impression than individual items—a swirl of draped layers in mostly dark colors, some grey that used to be black, a long, out-of-shape skirt, a red shawl, a turquoise scarf, a huge overstuffed bag, big clompy boots. Always a hat, a beret, a toque, a fedora.

She was loud, arguing with the secretary. Are you kidding? No one yells at the secretary. Is she crazy, alienating her like that?

Who is she? I asked another student. Oh her, that's Barbara, she said. Manic-Depressive. A roll of the eyes, an explanation, a dismissal. Another sip of coffee and down the hall while Barbara rants in the office.

Dismissed. Crazy Lady. Everyone avoided her. Even me. I was having a hard-enough time on my own, I didn't need any guilt by association. And she was kind of scary, edge-of-the-roof scary. I avoided her as if it were contagious. And it is contagious, isn't it, madness?

In Fourth Grade

In fourth grade, the teacher asks us to write down what our goals are in life. I don't even have to think about it. I want to know everything, I write. When the teacher comes by and looks at what I've written, she chuckles. I look at the words. *I want to know everything*. They don't seem funny to me.

What's Happening?

It is so much easier to write about mania, because with mania, there's always something happening. Who wants a story where nothing is happening? And yet that is the reverse side of this fabric that is my life, the erotic and its opposite, the life force and the creeping death. People like to use the term "downward spiral," but that is too active for depression. Mania is sometimes a dizzying out-of-control spiral of agitation; depression is the lying down of desire.

Crying all the time is bad, but at least it's something. You can say, Jeez, I'm crying all the time, I better do something about that. But depression is not-doing. Nothing.

There's this old joke about the philosophy student who asks, Who am I? The answer comes back: Who's asking? With depression that who is so deeply buried it doesn't notice that nothing's happening. It doesn't get bored and look for something to do. Oh, sweet boredom, that lets us know we are alive.

Jungle Road

I am driving home from night class, down what my son will later call Jungle Road because of how the trees loom, the way their branches hang over the car as we drive, the calls of jays, the drones of cicadas. That is years ahead of us. Tonight I am driving home alone. It's late, the high beams weave back and forth with the curves, the trees are dark—if I turn off the lights I will be lost in them. I am driving fast, taking each curve way to the outside, and I come to the walls, walls made of stone and brick, that line the road just before it opens out into the bright lights of Route 20. I think, It would be so nice to drive into that wall, that one there, the old-fashioned stone wall without mortar. I could just rip right through and be done with it. But at the last minute I turn. I think of my son, sleeping in his crib. He expects me in the morning as sure as sunrise. I turn the wheel. I come to a full stop before entering the traffic. I use my blinker before turning left onto the island. I drive down the dirt road. I make it home.

Blackouts

My mother told me about how in World War II they would have black-outs. All the lights would be put out, the shades drawn. No light from inside, no light escaping to the outside.

I blacked out, people would say about their drunken nights, never taking responsibility for their actions, I thought. Liars, I thought.

I was certain of my memory. I could remember entire conversations ver-batim. I could read *Harper's Magazine* lists once and recite them aloud. I could find the exact place on the exact page where I'd read something, some fact I needed, some quote I loved.

Some people say they can't remember their childhoods. But I am more like Flannery O'Connor, who said that if you've made it to age five, you have more than enough to write about for your entire life. I can remember flashes from infancy, my grandmother's nightie, the round TV screen on our little set, rolling potatoes around on the linoleum floor. The more I remember, the more I remember. My mother sitting at the piano crying in her silky brown maternity dress, my arm in an ice-cube tray after going through the wringer on the washing machine.

I have always trusted my memory. I enjoyed it when my brother read a story of mine, based on stories my grandmother told about a boy named

Stanley who liked to dance. I combined that story with a later Stanley, who once leaned against the telephone pole near my house and sang softly to himself, "My name is Stanley." My brother remembered that addition as part of my grandmother's story, and I was glad that it fit so seamlessly into that narrative, but also that the storytelling could fool him into remembering something that hadn't really happened. It never occurred to me that I wasn't immune from that. Or that, just like remembering something that hadn't happened, I might actually forget things that had.

"Guess who's bi?" I enter it as a subject line on an email to an ex after my diagnosis. In the body of the note, I say, "polar, that is." Next week when we have lunch she says that it doesn't surprise her, she knew something was up when I tipped over the dining room table during an argument that time.

What time? What table?

You don't remember that? she says. I shake my head while she tells me how in an argument with my ex-husband, I'd pushed the massive pine table over with all its plates and cups and silverware, books and papers, and how the cat had yelped and scattered the newspapers as it jumped off onto the sofa. I am totally silenced. This is some other person she's talking about.

Who cleaned up? I ask.

We both did, she says.

I wonder if that's why she left me. Did I do stuff like that often? I don't even want to ask her.

There's a lot I don't remember, apparently. I think of all those times people seem angry at me, and I don't know why. More evidence mounts up. People tell me things I don't remember. Sometimes it flashes by, I can almost remember. Sometimes, nothing.

Blackouts, I've been having blackouts. For most of my life, probably. I am not the person I thought I was. And if that's true, who am I?

Voices

There is nowhere that can be quiet enough because I am carrying these conversations inside my head. I don't know who they are, these voices, but they are not mine. Murmuring, murmuring, like in a theatre hall before the concert begins—I strain to hear the words, but I can't, it's just an undercurrent, murmuring, murmuring, with waves that come and go.

I can't write this because I'm afraid they will begin. I will have to be quiet as I whisper this to you. Sometimes the voices get louder, but no more comprehensible. It's not that they are speaking a different language, it's just that everyone is speaking at once. Chattering, chattering.

I remember when I realized how big the inside of my head is. The entire universe somehow fits inside. If I go to the center of my mind, the edges are infinite. So where does this echo come from?

I carry the voices around for days, for weeks, decades. I'm exhausted from listening. I try to hear what they're saying, but I can't, I never can. This is a party I can't walk away from. These guests were not invited. They are intruders—they come and go whenever they want. My mind is their crash pad.

The Bad Mother

The Wicked Witch of the West would have been a relief. When I was a kid, we'd all seen *The Wizard of Oz*, and everyone knew all the lines by heart. All that "beautiful wickedness." But that's not what it's like, being the bad mother.

We know her mostly in her disguise as the evil stepmother in all the fairy tales—the mother who makes you do all the chores, who is jealous of your beauty, who would kill you if it secured her power. But who would admit it was the mother herself? We are shocked by bad mothers. Joan Crawford, Sybil's terrible mother, crack whores, the woman who tied her two young children into their car seats before pushing them into the lake, and then blaming someone else . . . those are the crazy, bad mothers we see on the screen, in the media. Bad mothers, all of them.

I am not a bad mother, I am a good mother. I am a better mother than my mother. I want to avoid all her mistakes. I want to do everything right. I am good, I am nurturing. I'm the Earth Mother, feeding everyone, bringing the soothing cup of tea, the balm on any wound. I didn't have to tell myself this. I knew it with a sure conviction.

I am standing at the stove, making dinner. Tonight, it's chili. I sauté onions, garlic, peppers, ground beef. I open cans of tomatoes and black beans. I add the salt, the cumin, and chili powder. Meanwhile, the clock is ticking. It's close to six o'clock. He should be home soon; he gets out of work at five.

I peel the avocadoes, mash them in a bowl. I smash the garlic cloves in the mortar with salt and pound away at them. He's still not here. It shouldn't take that long. It's three minutes past six.

I cut the lemons, swear as the juice gets into a paper cut. Where the fuck is he? Why does he do this to me every day?

I stir the chili in a big cast-aluminum pot with a wooden spoon, a thick, hand-crafted spoon I bought in Bar Harbor on vacation. My favorite spoon. I stir faster. The sauce splashes on my hand. Goddamit. Fucking shit. I scream and bang the pot with the spoon, which breaks with a loud crack and flies over my head.

When my son comes into the kitchen, I'm at the sink, running cold water on my hand. He's heard the crash and the yelling. When I see his face, his scared eyes and trembling chin, I want him not to be scared, so I start to laugh. I drop the handle of the spoon into the sink, link eyes with him, as if it is a shared joke. I didn't know my own strength, I say. He laughs with me, as I fall against the counter, dizzy, liberated from my anger.

Every night my son endured some crisis while I made dinner. Ranting was, I thought, a normal venting of frustration. I even defended it, proudly telling people my family was not afraid of expressing anger.

Every night my husband told me that I shouldn't expect him until six-thirty. But somehow, when six o'clock came, the rage kicked in. One night I kicked out the bottom of the screen door. Just turned from the stove and kicked, and again, was surprised by my own strength when the metal panel crumpled. I am terrified by my own violence as I write this.

One morning my son tells me he's supposed to bring cookies or brownies to school. But it's okay, he says. They won't mind if I don't. How could you forget to ask me to bake something? And now I don't have time before work. I am banging around the kitchen again, trying to get everything together before we go out the door.

But it's not that he's forgotten. He wants the cookies and he doesn't. Mostly he wants me not to be mad. He is trying to protect himself, but there is no protection, because I yell at him for not telling me. I want to want to make the cookies. I want to be that kind of mother.

Sometimes I knew I'd gone over the top. I remember pounding on my husband's chest as he held my hands and asked me what I was so angry about. I don't know, I don't know, I sobbed, until I got tired and stopped the pounding, while he held my arms and hugged me until I relaxed.

I felt helpless against it. As if I were possessed. Then I would forget, though not really—I could remember an incident if we were talking about it, but always as something funny, hilarious, even—the day Ma broke the spoon, kicked out the door, slammed a pile of dishes into the sink where they all split down the middle as if struck by lightning. Individual incidents. Normal. Not a daily barrage of crazy rage. Not the bad mother.

Exceptional Children

I spend my time at school teaching the other kids fractions. I move from one desk to the next, mirroring the teacher across the room. At home I am learning decimals from my father. He is teaching me how to use his slide rule. After fractions, I'll go to the office and make copies for the teacher on the mimeo machine and run notes from the principal to different classrooms.

I don't mind this. All my learning happens outside of school anyway. When I was little my grandmother sent me outside to watch the grass grow. Since then, it's become a habit, this watching the world. I spend hours watching grasshoppers and ants, examining the stalks and flowers of grass, smelling pine sap, following toads, admiring the colors of the sky.

At the bookmobile, I've just gotten permission to take out adult books. My mother had to write me a special note. I am reading *Mice, Men and Molecules*, *Rebecca*, and *The Three Pillars of Zen*, which I don't understand but chose because I recognized the word *Zen*. There is a world out there, I know. Someone writes these books.

I live in a large extended family of cousins, grandparents, and siblings, in an island neighborhood with packs of kids. I don't tell anyone but my father about the books I read in private. Does anyone else wonder about things? Why are we here? Does the universe have edges? What happens when we die? What makes a sunset? And why do I feel happy and sad and full and open all at the same time when I hear certain music or see the Milky Way for the first time?

My eight-year-old grandson tells me about the new summer camp he's going to. I can study rocketry, woodworking, stage design, and pond life, he tells me, his hands expressing the vast possibilities he feels. I like it, he says. It's full of kids like me. When I smile, he says, no, really Memere, they're kids like me. I know, I tell him. I was one of those kids, too.

One day on the bus ride home from school, I see the sign. Exceptional Children Can Be Helped. I am so relieved. I tear off one of the coupons and bring it home. When I give it to my mother, she reads it, then looks at me puzzled.

I found it on the bus, I say. Uh-hunh, she says. But why did you bring it home? I read it to her.

Exceptional. Children. Can. Be. Helped. I look up, expecting to see light dawning, but she still looks puzzled. Well, I'm exceptional, I say.

Yes, you are, she laughs. But that's not what this means. This is about children who are slow, who need help. I think of the special room for kids like my cousin Doreen. There's no special room for kids like me.

The Twirling Skirt

It's my birthday and I get to open the big box. It will be a dress for Easter, I know, that's what I always get in the big box on my birthday. But inside the box there is a skirt with metallic gold thread, black velvet, and small pink flowers on a cream background. It's a circle skirt. It has crinoline underneath, which is scratchy, but I don't care because it's so beautiful.

I try it on, and it fits perfectly. Not like my school dresses that are always too big and too long so I can grow into them. It is a magic skirt, and I am beautiful wearing it. I wear it all day long. It is a twirling skirt, and I spin and spin, watching its colors spinning with me. I am a kaleidoscope, filled with light, I am a whirling star, a heavenly body, a galaxy with outspread arms.

On Monday, I get to wear it to school, and I twirl in the schoolyard in front of all my friends. I will wear it every day, this beautiful skirt. But I don't get to wear it to school every day because it is new and has to be saved for special. But special only happens once in a while, and I wear it only two more times before I am too big and it is too small.

The twirling skirt is passed down to my little sister, and because it's not new anymore, she wears it to school any time she wants, which is often. I watch my sister twirl and twirl in the beautiful skirt that no longer fits me. She knows it is magic and she is beautiful and she smiles like a spinning star.

Every year in late August when things are going on sale, my mother takes us shopping for school clothes. I don't want to go shopping. I know I'll never get the beautiful pink pullover sweater, but instead a sensible navy-blue cardigan. My mother has very clear ideas of what I should wear. Plaid dresses with white collars. Red plaid, blue plaid, green plaid.

I'm careful when I choose something because I know she will say, Well . . . I don't know. You'll be the one who has to wear it. And I will put back the dress with the lace insert, the grey with the pink pinafore, and choose another plaid, one I know my mother will like.

My sister chooses a Kelly green dress with black velvet ribbons. I gasp. My mother hates Kelly green. But my sister dances around in front of the mirror, and my mother laughs and gets her the dress. Then my sister picks out a purple dress. Look, she tells my mother, it won't get stained from blueberries. Last year she dropped blueberry cobbler from the school lunch onto her light blue dress, and the purple never came out. My mother laughs again. That's true, she says, and my sister goes home with two dresses she loves and I come home with my three plaid ones.

My mother picks out saddle shoes that make my skinny legs look like Olive Oyl in the Popeye cartoons. The shoes are heavy on my feet. I can't run fast or dance. I clomp around on the carpet at the shoe store to dramatize the problem. Pick up your feet, she says. On the first day of school, she takes a picture. Smile, she says, but it is hard to smile in saddle shoes.

When I'm going into fourth grade my mother says it's time to go shopping for clothes. I tell her, if you buy me saddle shoes I won't go to school. I mean it, I say. Everyone has pixie shoes, and if I have to wear Olive Oyl shoes I will die. She doesn't say anything, but at the shoe store, she walks past the saddle shoes, to the display of pixie shoes, pointed and delicate with thin round laces.

At home, I open the box every day, pull back the white crinkly paper, just to look at them, black and dainty. I am amazed at how easy it was. I was ready for a fight. I had dug in my heels.

Later, in my twenties, when I'm working at an office job at the university, I buy myself two skirts. I call them the life skirt and the death skirt. One is a black A-line with black piping swirls across the hips. The other is made of overlapping strips of gold and green and pink and black, sewn in a chevron down the front. Not a twirling skirt, but a beautiful one. I wear them to work instead of jeans and T-shirts. I wear them with high-heeled boots that reach my knees. I wear them any time I want.

Crazy Talk I

She is large and disheveled. If you met us both on the street, she is the one you would peg as crazy. Her hair is uncombed. She wears an oversize man's white shirt, open over a greyed knit top that has seen better days. This is a clinic for people without insurance. Maybe she thinks she doesn't have to dress up for us.

She laughs at everything I say, as if I am there for her amusement. There's a name for that. Hebephrenia, after the Greek goddess, Hebe. I refrain from telling her this.

Can I write that down? she asks me frequently, and scribbles in her book. Her laugh is loud and raucous like a cross between a cockatoo and a hyena. I fall into the role she's cast me in and entertain her with frivolous stories and wisecracks.

When I need her to fill out a form for my disability, she doesn't remember who I am.

white
pines
reach out
extend their
healing arms
and small birches
grow at the edges
leaning
toward sun
oaks are plentiful
but there are
no mother trees here
wider than we are tall
there are
pricker bushes but where
are the berries?
which of these mushrooms
can I eat? which roots
will cure wounds,
which kill? Avoid
them all, then,
become afraid
of everything

The Death Turnpike

In the 1930s, when my mother was a girl, her sisters would come in a rowboat to take her to the island where they lived in small, winterized cottages that had been vacation cottages until the island became too crowded and unfashionable. It was cheap housing for the poor during the Great Depression.

Before the cottages, the island had been a park. My grandmother remembered riding the trolley from her home on Shrewsbury Street in Worcester down to the lake, where they boarded a ferryboat from the Marina on Route 9. Families went there to picnic and swim. At one point there was a racetrack for horses or dogs. Our house was on one leg of what had been that track.

Before we lived there, before the park or the cottages or the racetrack, the island had been part of what the Nipmuc people called *Quinsigamond*, which people said meant the pickerel fishing place. The lake is still called Quinsigamond, and when I was a girl, there were a lot of pickerel still, those small, pond-size barracuda with sharp teeth and lots of tiny bones and sweet flesh.

Sometime after the Hurricane of '38, when the community house was blown down, never to be rebuilt, the state filled in some land on the south part of the island and built a highway. They made two small bridges, so small a passing motorist would barely notice them, that connected the island to Shrewsbury on the east and Worcester on the west.

The highway had as many names as a character from a Russian novel, only none of them were affectionate. Some just told you where it was or where it went to, or what number the state gave to it—The

Boston-Hartford Turnpike, the Southwest Cutoff, Route 20. One described its character—The Death Turnpike.

There were many ways off the island, if you had a boat. Three if you were walking—the two ends of the horse track that led onto the Cutoff, and an old dirt road that crossed a dam on the other side of the island, with the big lake on one side, Flint Pond on the other. But if you were driving there was no way to avoid the Cutoff.

It was a dangerous place. From the very first days of its being open, people began dying on its three lanes, one lane going in each direction, with a middle one for passing. You can see how that would be a problem. Two cars making the switch to the middle lane at the same time. Or misjudging their timing. Or black ice or rain or drunkenness, or maybe the lack of traffic lights. The Death Turnpike, it was baptized in blood.

But we didn't call it that. To us it was the Cutoff, and we weren't allowed there. Every day at noon we'd hear the firehouse whistle blow from the bottom of the hill, calling us all in for lunch. By the time we were twelve we could ride our bikes down to the firehouse, and to Jim's Gas Station next door where we'd put air into our tires and watch the trucks go by. Next to Jim's was the Edgemere Diner, where we'd get hot cocoa in winter and, later, breakfast at midnight with jukeboxes at each table, our last stop on a date.

When we were old enough, we walked to the Spa. This was not a place you went to for beauty treatments, with big towels and fancy drinks. It was a small grocery with a soda fountain, comic books, cigarettes, and batteries. We didn't actually spend our time in the Spa, we had to buy things to stay inside. Going to the Spa meant hanging outside, watching the traffic go by, smoking cigarettes, meeting up with friends, and deciding what to do next.

We watched a meteor flash through the sky from there, one that ultimately landed in New Jersey. My first dog, Prince, died there, and Mrs. LaMoine's husband. Farther down by the bridge, my cousin Sonny died in a crash. Neighbors and relatives and people we didn't know. The trucks didn't slow down. Once, when I was eight months pregnant, my belly touching the steering wheel, a truck ran me off the road—I barely had time to make a sharp right onto Lakeside drive—one of the two legs of the horse track that ran into Route 20.

One day, in my early twenties, I was driving to my parents' house with my two-year-old son. The Cutoff was full of trucks as usual, and I thought nothing of it when I pulled over to the middle lane to take my left turn onto the island. Nothing until I looked in the rear-view mirror and saw that a semi had pulled into the lane behind me and had no intention of stopping. Another semi was passing me on the right, and a third was coming head-on toward me in lane number three. There was no way I could make a left turn in time.

I remember seeing my son, who'd been tossed to the floor. I thought it was over for both of us, and grieved his short life. And then I felt it, that peace people talk about. "Death is the best high, that's why they save it for last"—who said that? Jim Morrison? Who knows? But I felt it—euphoria, peacefulness, total acceptance.

I watched the semi that was approaching me veer off into a yard and nearly into the lake. The truck behind me squeezed by inches from my face, scraping the chrome, the door handle, and the mirror off the car. And then time speeded up again, and I reached for my son. I could see people outside Jim's Gas Station watching, but I was too dazed to do anything. Finally, one of the men came over and tapped at the window. He motioned me to open the door, since there was no longer a handle on the outside, and when I did, he walked me over to Jim's, then went back to get the car. That's what I remember—that moment of peace and the truck scraping against the car. I couldn't believe we were alive.

The man who'd walked me from my car looked back at me, and we locked eyes before he left. I recognized his face, but I didn't know from where. I never saw him again. Thank you. I remember saying thank you.

We were safe. We were lucky. It should have been over. I should have appreciated the fact that we were alive, the beauty of each ordinary day—isn't that what's supposed to happen? It didn't happen that way.

It was that moment of peace. You're not supposed to get that moment of peace unless you die. But I'd had it, that intense understanding that it was all alright. I accepted Death and then lived. Now Death was gunning for me.

At first it was just fear on the highway. Cringing as a semi flew by. Who wouldn't cringe after being surrounded by semis, after having one fly by six inches from my face? The Hartford Turnpike, Route 20, the Death Turnpike, no longer went to Hartford, but merged instead with Route 84, where the trucks traveled even faster. You could feel the air suck toward them as they flew past, tires whistling. My husband's family lived in the Hartford area, and each time we got on the road, the anxiety would begin. What started as cringes escalated into gasps, covering my head and hunching my shoulders against a crash, then finally trying to get out of the car, away from danger.

I tried to open the car door—*I have to get out, I have to get out*—and my husband swerved as he pulled me back toward him, trying to reason with me. You can't get out, we're going sixty-five miles an hour. *I know, I know, but I have to get out.* Not once, but every time we drove to Hartford.

My son was in the back seat, five, six years older now and terrified of his mother trying to jump out of the car, but nevertheless I had to escape. Danger. Everywhere danger. In the car, out of the car. No moment of peace. Just Death. Everywhere.

Life in the Fast Lane

Am I Paranoid, or Are They Really Out to Get Me?

Sometimes people move too goddam slow.

I'm cooking dinner. My husband is sous-chef, helping, working around me. Get me that colander, I say. When I am in chef mode, everything is a command.

Okay, he says. But he is doing something else, something he wants to finish first, like dry his hands, or put down the knife he's been using to slice onions. I roll my eyes.

And then he oh, so, s-l-o-w-l-y moseys across the kitchen That is what he does, moseys. He has always been a mosey-er. I used to think it was charming. Now he moseys across the kitchen. His moseying is even worse today. He opens one cupboard door, looks forever into its depths, moves a few pans. Then shuts the door. I am going crazy here. The pasta is going to overcook.

For chrissakes, can't you get the damn colander?

He is walking through molasses. He opens another cupboard, bends slowly to gaze inside, finally reaches in, he is straining my patience now, hesitates, H-E-S-I-T-A-T-E-S, and drags out the colander as if it's a heavy cast iron pan. He straightens—every movement in slo-mo. How can he be this way? Why did I marry him?

Instead of just handing me the colander, which I so obviously need, he takes a dishcloth and swirls and swirls and swirls it around the colander, adding precious minutes to the process, then starts slowly across the kitchen.

Nobody can move this slowly unless they are doing it on purpose. Why would he do that? He is doing this on purpose, to punish me, or mock me, or who knows why.

I am seething. I am shaking my head. I am yelling at him to stop the shit and get his ass moving. You are such an asshole, I shout. Give me the damn colander. I grab it, dump the pasta, which is miraculously still firm and not a pot of mush, into the colander, drain it, slam the pot back on the stove, drizzle olive oil with a vengeance, grate the Parmagian cheese, sprinkle salt in a circle, grab the pepper mill, and grind fresh pepper, the smell of which makes me even angrier for some reason. I slam the serving bowl onto the table, along with the salad. Dinner's ready, I shout.

Now my son is in on it. He's only eight. He should be running down the stairs, but even his descent is slow. They are in it together. It's a conspiracy. They are doing it just to irritate me.

This is what is called paranoid ideation. Thinking that someone is out to get you. This, my therapist says, is when I become psychotic.

Psychotic? That is a serious word. I think about this a lot. It's scary. How do I know what is real? What does it mean to be paranoid? I think of the old line from the sixties. Is it paranoid when they're really out to get you?

We are in Friendly's, my daughter-in-law, Marci, and my grandsons, Joey, who is four, and Adam, who is still a toddler. We sit in a booth. The place is almost empty, yet no one seems to notice us. Adam doesn't want to sit, and Marci walks with him up and down the aisle. Still no waitress.

In the next aisle, between all the empty booths, a waitress is mopping the floor. I take a deep breath, shake my head and look away. Hasn't anyone trained these women? Doesn't the customer come first? Why the hell doesn't she stop that mopping and come over and take our order?

Finally another waitress comes to our booth. I try to be polite, but she is getting confused by our order, and repeats it several times. We each order a meal that comes with an ice cream dessert.

It takes a long time before our meals come. Joey has crayons and a place mat, and he is coloring. I lean over and he asks me to color, too.

We color for a long time. The entire mat is colored, so we turn it over and draw pictures.

The lights are getting brighter. Everything is loud. I'm getting that dark shrinking of my vision, that tightening in my scalp that tells me a migraine is coming on. Still the food hasn't come. If I don't eat soon, the headache will slam in.

I'm finding it hard to breathe when our lunch finally arrives. I am sure I ordered grilled cheese with tomato, but she brings a fish sandwich instead. I make a face and start to eat. It isn't that I don't like fish sandwiches, it just isn't what I ordered. That waitress didn't like me. She heard what I said to Marci about the customer coming first, so she deliberately messed up my order.

I tell Marci this, and she says, Don't be silly. But I know I'm not being silly.

I'm done eating before everyone else, and have to wait for them to finish. Joey and Adam seem to be taking longer than usual to finish their chicken and French fries, and even Marci seems to be taking her sweet time, sipping her iced tea like it's a day at the beach.

Finally we are done. Now we wait for the waitress. She apparently takes the word "wait" very seriously. When she comes, she takes our orders for ice cream. She seems to get everything the first time, which is a relief. But then she doesn't come back. Adam and I are agitated. This is just unbearable.

When she arrives with the ice cream, my hot fudge sundae has chocolate ice cream instead of vanilla. This is two mistakes in one meal. Now I know it's on purpose. She apologizes. Right. And then sashays, I swear she sashays, down the aisle.

Marci is dressing the boys, we are leaving. I will pick up my ice cream at the counter on the way out. We put on the boys' coats, hats, and mittens, pick up our bags, gloves, and hats. Let's go, let's go, I am saying the whole time.

When we get to the counter my sundae isn't done yet. There is something wrong with the machine. Why do they need a machine? What machine? There is a different waitress scooping vanilla into a to-go bowl.

She is going slowly, like everything in this stupid place. I can't stand any more. There are three waitresses standing around her, talking. About me.

Can you hurry it up? I say. One of the waitresses looks up at me and says, She's just learning. I know she's lying. She goes back to talking with the others.

How many waitresses does it take to make a hot fudge sundae? I ask.

Is this a riddle? one of them slings back at me. The gauntlet has been thrown.

Why are you doing this? What have I ever done to you? Just get me the damn sundae so I can get out of here.

The waitress suddenly goes into double speed, and whisks the sundae onto the counter. See, I knew they were doing it on purpose. Here's your damn sundae, she says. I'm never coming here again, I say. Good! she says. As I walk to the door, I hear Joey ask, Mama, why is Memere in such a hurry?

This is my reality check. Joey is four. There is something wrong with what just happened. My anger is all out of proportion. Everyone is looking at me funny. I am the crazy lady at Friendly's.

I agree, finally, to take meds. I never want my grandsons to see me like that again. Later, Marci tells me we were only in Friendly's for about half an hour, tops. It felt like three times that to me. Not normal. Something's wrong. But paranoia? Really? Isn't that thinking people are out to get you when you have no evidence to support it?

Consider: You are making dinner, when suddenly everyone around you is moving ridiculously slowly. You are the only one moving at a normal speed. They don't respond to any comments you make about them moving their butts a little faster. They just keep moving along like they've got all day, and get surlier each time you try to hurry them up.

How would you make sense of this? For that is the crux of it. Isn't that what we all do, try to make sense of our experience? If, in fact, everyone were moving slowly, what would you think?

Maybe you'd ask yourself, is this a joke? But if you test that hypothesis (move your butts) and there's no response but resistance? Okay, that's not it. Then why? After another try they start scowling or telling you they are going as fast as they can, when obviously that is not true. Anyone could see they would have to put effort into moving that slowly.

Why would they do that? If it's not a joke, and they are all doing it together, what's going on? If it's not a joke, then what? Could it be they are trying to annoy you for some reason? Are they trying to give you some message? If so, what? And why won't they just tell you instead of going through this elaborate pantomime?

Whatever is going on, it is well-coordinated, they are all in it together, and you are out of the loop. They are doing it to get a rise out of you, isn't that the only possible conclusion? Well, no. They could all be holograms in slo-mo, or they could all have been replaced by aliens who haven't quite learned Terrans' sense of time, or they could all have taken some kind of drug, like Quaaludes only more so, or maybe they have become zombies—their minds eaten by TV and video games, but no, that's crazy thinking, funny, but not applicable. Think Occam's Razor—the most likely explanation is the simplest one. In this case, given the evidence, the simplest explanation is that they are doing this to get to you. But you don't know why.

Paranoia. Psychologists, therapists, people generally agree that it is crazy thinking, that it is the ideation that is the problem. But if people were in fact going slow all around you, everyone at once, the thoughts are not crazy at all. It is just problem solving applied to an impossible situation. Because here is the thing, it is not the thinking that's wrong, it's the perception.

No one ever asked me, in all the years I was in therapy, if things ever slowed down, if people ever seemed to be moving or talking particularly slowly. Instead they asked me if I ever had racing thoughts. No, I think fast all the time, I joked.

The only time I had racing thoughts was when I'd drunk way too much caffeine, in which case my heart was pounding, my hands felt trembly, and, yes, my thoughts were moving pretty fast. But people weren't in slo-mo when that happened. I knew I was caffeinated. I didn't need to find any other meaning in it. My thinking was fine. My perception was accurate.

I remember moving in slo-mo once, when I was very stoned. I walked down a short hill to the pizza place, and it took forever, every step a giant one, leading with that big foot like in the R Crumb comics. I knew I was stoned, I enjoyed the perception of time slowing down. I didn't question it or try to explain it. I just smoked a joint, I'm stoned. Enjoy the moment.

But what if your perceptions are wrong? What if time speeds up, and you have no way of knowing? What if nobody says, Slow down—you're moving way too fast?

I see it as if in a movie. There's a woman in the kitchen. She is chopping vegetables, carrots maybe, mushrooms. There are other people around her, moving in slo-mo. She is the only one moving in real time.

Next shot: Everyone is making dinner. Everyone is moving at a normal, relaxed pace. At the counter a woman is chopping vegetables. But her movement is speeded up, like in an old Keystone Cops movie. She doesn't seem to notice that she's moving way too fast.

So with no other explanation, I tried to make meaning of my perceptions, which were wrong, because, in fact, I was zipping along in the fast lane, way over the speed limit. But I didn't know that, my speedometer was broken. All those people are driving really slow . . .

Psychotic? I don't think so. Now when people go into slo-mo I know it's not them, I know I'm in the fast lane, I pay attention, I do what I need to do to slow down. I know it is my perception that is skewed. Explanation provided. Paranoia magically gone.

Meds

The med that the psychiatrist, my med doc, puts me on is dangerous. It can cause a severe skin rash. If you don't get to the hospital right away, he tells me, you can die.

I check my skin every few minutes. Every little itch, every discoloration—is that new, or did I always have that? Is that red blotch on my face something I should worry about? I lift up my shirt to check my belly. Isn't that where measles always starts? Maybe this rash is like measles, drawn to the heat.

When I go to the bathroom, I check my thighs, my knees. I check my armpits when I put on deodorant. I don't want to die from this fucking medicine I agreed to try. I hate medicine. I don't want to take any. I told the med doc that I'm very sensitive to drugs. He said to call him if I get the slightest rash.

What does the rash look like? I ask him over the phone.

Do you have a rash? he asks.

No. But what does it look like?

Don't worry, if you have it, you'll know. It's a very severe rash, you won't miss it. Remember you have lorazepam if you get too anxious.

Right. Then I'll be drugged and miss the damn rash. Or see it, and say, Oh, that's nothing to worry about. Go to sleep and wake up dead. Why did I ever agree to take these meds?

After four weeks, with no rash, Dr. B. ups the dosage. We'll go slowly with this. How are you feeling?

Okay. People have stopped moving in slo-mo.

That's good.

I don't feel like I'm not me. Maybe a clearer me.

Cheryl, meet Cheryl, he says.

I don't stop cycling. I'm still far from stable. But my head is above the current.

Arthur Lloyd

Arthur Lloyd is a bad boy. He's always in trouble. He locks the teacher in the closet. He doesn't do homework. He's absent on test days. He is two years older than everyone in my class. He causes a ruckus in the classroom almost every day. In the fall he leaves for weeks to go hunting in Maine, where his family is from, like my family a long time ago. I am a little awed by him. He isn't stupid like everyone says.

One day I'm out in the swamp near his house looking for frogs, when he comes by. He stops and watches me. There's a frog out there, he says, pointing with his chin, and suddenly there is a frog where I hadn't seen one before. It turns out he knows lots of stuff, stuff I want to know. He knows all the frogs and can do all their sounds. He knows which clumps of eggs will be frogs and which will be toads or salamanders. He can be quieter than anyone I know.

He shows me holes where snakes live, and holes in the tree made by woodpeckers. He shows me the difference between pines and spruce, and how to suck nectar from lilac flowers. He shows me paths I don't know about, and rubs jewelweed on my calf after I trip into a patch of poison ivy.

We love crows because they love to play, and after he tells me they have their own language we sit for hours listening, trying to learn it. I can only make the alarm call, but he can make a chattering call, and a strange hiccup caw that makes me laugh. We go out in the rowboat and he scares me by talking about the false bottom of the pond and the huge bass who live under its slimy clumps of mud.

The teachers don't get it, but my father does. Smart kids know who the other smart kids are. For teachers smart sometimes comes in only one flavor. He learns from his grandfather, my father says. I love his grandfather. I deliver papers to his house, and he gives me hot cocoa in the winter.

When I get a microscope for Christmas, I can't wait to look at swamp water with Arthur, but in the spring he goes trucking in his father's semi, and when he comes back I don't know until one day I find him kissing Donna in the woods. I thought we would be friends forever, but all of a sudden, I'm just a kid, and he's found more interesting things to do.

shades

she stays in bed most of the day. sometimes she gets up to get something to eat. she forgets to bathe or brush her teeth. her hair is uncombed. oily strands tangle around her face and shoulders.

the shades are drawn because the light hurts her eyes. the brightness is like a knife, a shaft of light that can bring on a migraine. she needs to hide her face from this furnace of light. it's as if she's just walked from a dark room into sunshine, except her eyes never get used to the light. everyone thinks that if she just opens the shades she will feel better. she needs some sunshine, that's what they say.

if she is unhappy she doesn't know it. sometimes she cries, but it is beyond unhappiness. she is curled up in a corner, holding her knees close to her chest. it is just tears. she is crying. she is the crying. there is no thought. she doesn't know why. she doesn't even know to question why.

sometimes she doesn't have the energy to sit and hold her knees, she just lies in bed and in her mind's eye she sees herself, sitting, rocking, rocking.

The Bra Thing

It's when I'm washing that my grandmother notices my breasts. There are dark circles around them where I've avoided washing them. Why aren't you washing your chest, she says, and takes a wash cloth in hand. She scrubs the dirt from my chest, and I cry until my mother comes in and stops her.

She takes the cloth from my grandmother's hands and washes me gently. She looks carefully at my chest. I think she's looking for more dirt, and hang my head. Then she reaches out and presses her hand against each breast. She looks worried. What's the matter, Ma? I look at my chest. That's when I notice my nipples are sticking out. Oh, nothing, she says and smiles. She starts vigorously washing my neck.

Then comes the poking and prodding. I'm called inside from playing to the living room where my mother has me lift my shirt for inspection by my three aunts. My mother is worried about something. I am impatient to get back outside, and look at the ceiling while they discuss whether my "whosies," as Aunt Doris calls them, are okay. I don't know what they are worried about. They can't decide, and Aunt Marie says take her to the doctor. So my mother does. Instead of my cheek, which he pinches hard each time we visit, Dr. Tomaiolo pinches my nipples. Then he smiles at my mother. Totally normal, he says, and before I can lower my shirt, he pinches a nipple again, as if it's a joke.

In school, I'm wearing my favorite tangerine sweater, cotton knit, with a band of white down the center. I'm hurrying to get my math done so I can get to the library at the back of the room before recess, when the shortest boy in the class walks by and says, Hey, Cheryl, what have you got under your shirt? I don't get it. Nothing, I say, and look up at him. What does he mean? He sniggers at me, not looking at my face, but lower. I follow his eyes to my chest and see the two little peaks and feel ashamed, but I don't know why. I haven't done anything. I hunch my shoulders. Always before I liked him. Now I hate him. How can a boy a whole head shorter than me make me feel small?

I tell my mother about it, and she says it's time to get a bra. Don't worry, she says. The bra will fix everything. I don't want a bra. They look uncomfortable and weird. I tell Terry, my best friend. She knows just what to do. She got a bra a couple of months ago. How come you didn't tell me, I ask her. She just shrugs her shoulders and laughs. We are the Fat and Skinny of the neighborhood. Fat and Skinny have a race, up and down the pillowcase. I am the skinny one, all arms and legs. She is the fat one, all round and cuddly. Maybe that's why I didn't notice.

That Saturday, Terry and I take the bus downtown. She, who usually follows my lead, walks ahead of me, down into the bowels of Filene's Basement, where we usually scavenge through shoes, scarves, gloves, and hats. I look longingly at the bins of wool and leather, but she won't stop. She's on a mission. We walk through aisles of underwear and bras so big I could wear them as hats. I'm thinking of that when she stops in front of a saleswoman and tells her I need to be measured. Oh, no. She didn't tell me about this part. One more person touching me. I look down a side aisle for an escape route. But Terry is looking so proud and happy that I lift my arms as asked and really it's not so bad.

The woman finds me a bra. When I put it on the straps are too long, and Terry shows me how to adjust them, how the hooks and eyes work in back. When I look in the mirror, I'm still the skinny little girl, and the white bra is ugly. But it covers up my breasts, it'll do the job. Terry says I have to buy two, so I do. She is the expert.

Finally it's over, and we go our usual route to Woolworth's and Kresge's looking at all the jewelry and umbrellas, the fake fingernails and eyelash curlers. We get slices of pizza and walk over to the Common. Everything is the same, except it isn't. Under our shirts we're wearing bras, *brassieres*, and we both know this is the end and the beginning of something.

I Am in Love with Rita Moreno

We go to see *West Side Story*, my best friend and I. We are twelve and this is our first grown-up movie. It opens with a shot of New York City and a sharp whistle. This is real. This is a neighborhood. I am swept away by the music, the jazzy beat, the dancing down streets, under the highway, in parking garages. I will tell my parents the soundtrack is all I want for Christmas. For years, my sister and I will sing the songs, dance in the kitchen while washing dishes.

On the way home, my friend tells me she is in love with Bernardo, who do I love? I don't know, I am still dancing with the women on the roof. Our hands meet over our heads, and now my arm is around her waist. We lock eyes and walk in a circle around each other. Now we are swishing our skirts high, stamping our feet, doo doo Dah dit dah, Dah dit dah, DUM DUM DUM, Dah dit dit Dah dit dit Dum d'Daaaah.

I will be her skirt, I will be her shoes, I will be the flower she wears in her hair, the shawl she wraps around her shoulders. I am in love with Rita Moreno.

Crazy Talk II

There is no such thing as a nervous breakdown, he says. I have been crying for weeks and I can't stop. He leans back in his chair, pushing slightly away from his desk. This is the extent of his intake examination before he assigns me to a therapist, who happens to be his wife.

I meet her at their house. The stairs to her basement office are next to the kitchen, which is several times the size of mine, with granite countertops, overhead racks with hanging copper pans, an island big enough to live on with a sink, two ovens that I can see, and a window with herbs growing that extends out behind another, bigger sink. When I compliment her on her kitchen, she says that I could have one like that. When I say, I don't think so, she asks why I think I don't deserve one.

Apparently she's unfamiliar with class analysis, it's all a matter of choice for her. Yes, I'm poor by choice, I want to say, but can't. I hate her and everyone like her.

She tells me my animosity towards her is about my mother. I admit, she does have curly red hair, but that is where the similarity ends. Still, it's true that I have dreams that I am driving to therapy with my mother in the back seat.

She tells me that my relationships with women are too intense. I don't know what to say, I am silenced. How can I come out to her? She doesn't even ask about my sexual preferences. I want to say, You're wrong, they're not intense enough, but I have no energy, no sense of humor.

We are always playing Alice in here—sometimes I am small and she is huge, other times she is tiny and receding into the distance. Rarely are we the same size.

We have been discussing a chronic illness that has had me in pain, with restricted movement for the past several years. We've talked about it before. One day I mention it and she says, Well, everyone gets sick sometimes, with a broken leg, or surgery. How long, exactly, were you ill?

Beautiful Doll

I was my mother's first child, full of promise, pretty with my hair done in Shirley Temple curls. My mother dressed me like a doll, in clothes she chose or made, and made me sit still while she set my hair in rags. I would suffer under her ungentle hands tugging the ends. My tears had no effect on this process. You have to suffer to be beautiful, she would tell me. The rags hurt to sleep on, pulled all night at my hair, and the lumps gave me a headache.

Oh, you beautiful doll, you great big beautiful doll, my mother sang to me, rocking me in her lap. I can't say I didn't like those times, my mother's arms around me, her warm body, the energy with which she rocked the chair. But I worried, did she not know I was a real girl, not a doll like Pinocchio? I liked to hear the other song, the one that went, *Put your arms around me, honey, hold me tight, huddle up and cuddle up with all your might.* I loved to cuddle, to be the real live girl. *I long to hold you but I'm afraid you'd break.* Oh, Oh, Oh, Oh, Oh, you beautiful doll.

The Ugly Year

So this is the ugly year. The hormones have really kicked in. They are over-flowing in the oil that slicks down my hair and the pimples that erupt on my face. I haven't figured out yet that I have to wash my hair every day. This is the year that I get glasses. For the past two years I've been going up to the board to write down assignments, and I've caught a few softballs with the top of my head, so now when I'm forced to play I walk way out beyond any possible outfield, almost into the woods that surround the ball field. The teacher starts hollering at me way before I stop and turn to face them. She can make me go to gym, but she can't make me stand in the way of a ball.

You'd think someone would have noticed I couldn't see. When I go downtown to pick up my glasses, it's a November afternoon. I go into the doctor's office through a world with soft edges, and come out into an evening of bright lights, pin points, sharp, with no rings around them. I can see people's faces. I can read signs.

I have no illusions. I examine myself in the mirror, the stringy hair, the pimples, the glasses. I look like Margaret in *Dennis the Menace* car-toons. At least I don't have those silly curls sitting on top of my head, though when my mother curls my hair into a pageboy, parted on the side, there is a roll of hair going all the way up one side of my head, caught in a barrette.

You're never going to make it on looks, I tell myself. I pull my hair back. It makes me look older, I think, and smarter. You'll have to do it with brains and personality. I think I can pull that off.

It's in this, my ugly year, that I decide I will be a courtesan. I have been reading *Camille*, and some other books that featured courtesans in India, and I've seen the movie *Gigi*. It seems to me that courtesan is a rational choice. The way I figure it is this. I'll get to read all the books I want, hang out with artists and musicians and thinkers, I'll get to have a *salon*, and though I know there is sex involved, I'm not worried about it. I hear my parents in bed, my mother's giggling, my father's low playful voice, so it can't be so bad. I figure there'll be a circle of adoring men, and I can just wave my arm and choose. My child, if I have one, will grow up with art and music, with interesting ideas in the air, not in a boring school.

There will be beautiful silks hanging draped from the ceilings in every color of the rainbow. There will be a hookah, which I've only seen in *Alice in Wonderland*, but I know it belongs in this room I am furnishing in my dream. There will be paintings on easels presented to me by artists, and flute music playing. We will eat exotic fruit and drink wine. It won't be boring. I will live far away from little league fields and gas stations. It will be beautiful.

I have been taught well. Women are not artists. It is never me painting the picture, never me composing the music, writing the books. I will do what I have to do to be in that *milieu*. *Milieu* is one of my favorite words. It's French, and I say it whenever I can get it into a conversation. I feel very comfortable in that *milieu*, I say to my father about the bookmobile. *Milieu* and *flamboyante*, a word I've heard my mother say. I know what she means when she describes women this way—they are flaming, they are beyond good taste, they are not boring.

It will be another twenty years before I know that not everyone pronounces this word as my mother does in French where it sounds so rich and alluring, that in English it sounds crass, with the accent on "boy," a syllable very different than the "bwa" sound of the French. I describe a woman to a friend, She's so, you know, *flamboyante*, I say. My friend laughs, a deep laugh from her belly. I can see her so clearly, she says, when you pronounce it in French. What do you mean, French? I ask.

I've got it down, this fantasy from old novels. I am crushed when I learn about whores. But they're different, I say. I won't be a whore, I'll be a courtesan. There's no longer a call for courtesans. Men don't want culture, nobody wants culture, they just want sex.

there are
brilliant berries
in the crazywoods
on vines that choke the trees
but still our eyes
are caught
we take them home
to dress the mantle
hang them on doors
next year they will
grow thick
in some new spot
or from old stumps
we've hacked
they should be gone
but in spring we find them
covered with bees
and here to stay

Krishna, My Love

When she spoke of it to him, he denied it. For some reason, this didn't seem unreasonable to her. She felt suddenly shy before him. She felt as if she herself had somehow committed a faux pas, that this was something that was not supposed to be mentioned, something she was not supposed to know. But somehow she had glimpsed another world, a deeper reality.

She had been there, she had seen the light around them, felt the world dropping away until it was just the light, the sacred. She had seen his face.

It took a lot of time before she'd mentioned it to him. How she knew who he was. How he didn't have to hide it from her. How she wouldn't tell anyone. How much she loved him.

What the fuck are you talking about? he said when she told him. His black hair draped over his shoulders and down his back, a dark mane. He sat on the sofa, pulled off his work shirt, wiped it over his chest.

I've seen your divinity, she said. I know who you are. Once again she could see him, blue-skinned, glowing.

Where is this coming from? I'm a Jew, for chrissakes. I'm not some blue god. And she'd gotten it finally. She wasn't supposed to know.

I'm sorry, she told him. I know I'm not supposed to know but I do.

Will you just drop it? he said.

At night he came to her and she felt that point of union expand until it was the whole universe. They were at the center of love, stars themselves, glowing orange, glowing turquoise. When she came back into herself, their bodies were filled with radiant light.

See that, she said.

Mmmmmmmmmm. What? he said.

The light.

Mmmmm you taste so good.

She watched him after that, waiting for the mask to slip.

Up north, they watched the northern lights, rippling greens and blues. Later he was the aurora inside her dark sky, colors of light rippling through her. Sometimes she was the goddess, glowing with her own light, and he in awe of her vastness. She took him in, and along with him, the universe she had birthed, and they floated together in the great fecund nothingness.

She is me, of course. When I recount this story in therapy, it is labeled delusional. It is a symptom of madness. I hear this with a great sense of loss. I still believe it happened, I tell my therapist. Yes, she says, a lot of patients feel that way.

I cannot live in a logical, dead, boring, accountant's world. I want to live in a world alive and full of magic and passion. If stabilizing this illness means that I have to define the world as nonmagical, nonsacred, I cannot do it.

I don't ever again want to have one of those mixed-states where I'm anxious and irritable, depressed and hypervigilant, all at the same time. I could've used a long stay in a cave at that time. So I stay on the meds. But I think of going off them almost every day. Compulsively active. Creative and mad.

I am afraid of never experiencing the numinous again. Of being cut off. Where is the boundary between madness and vision? Between living in a dead secular world and living in a numinous sacred universe?

Maybe it's been a gift as much as a curse, this way of being in the world. I've been the consort of a god, as well as a captive of poison in a jar of cranberry juice. I've created beauty. I've burst into song in restaurants with no sense of impropriety, told stories that made people lean over from other tables to listen. I have found god in puddles of paint. I have danced for wildflowers and to welcome the wind. I have been the object of curses, the victim of witchcraft. I have bound rapists with threads they could not break. Bears have walked through our bed as we made love, as we became bears with them. I give thanks, I feel blessed.

Here's what I think happens. There is a moment when I perceive the sacredness of the universe, of myself as part of that, merged with it so that all boundaries disappear. Everything is blossoming with meaning, with joy, with exquisite color and insight. I believe this sacredness is real, and that we are lucky when we have these moments. And then, because storying is what we humans do, I try to hang this experience on a narrative—whatever mythology seems to hold it. This is when what they call madness begins.

In the story "Yellow Woman," by Leslie Silko, a woman goes out and encounters a man who is mythic, a spirit lover. There is a sense of being in the old Yellow Woman stories, of her being Yellow Woman, and at the same time she is skeptical, a woman of the twentieth century. How much of what they call madness is a lack of the right story from my own culture to hold these moments of sacred sex? Only later do I understand that the bears who walked through our beds are from our own stories of the woman who married a bear, that marriage with the Land, with the sacred, more-than-human world.

There are stories around the world full of gods taking on human form. It is Krishna, the loving blue god, that I believe has taken over the body of my lover. I cannot be dissuaded in my belief. No matter how he denies it, I know who he is, I have seen his sacredness. He does not want me to know, but I do know. I have seen him in his glory, his blue skin bathed in light. I have expanded through the whole universe with him—stars float through us without harm, we are the body of the universe itself.

When I return, it is in stages—first a kind of gathering in from the great expanses into the compactness of a human body. And then there is language, and a knowing that I am human. And that is good. I become aware of my woman's body—I know that I am female, a woman. And that is good. Finally I feel myself as separate from my mate, an individual with a name.

It is a gradual coming back, and it is always surprising. The other reality is so much stronger, it is the real, and all this separateness the illusion.

For a moment, I am both in my body, and the body of the universe itself, but I cannot sustain that. I am reluctant to let go. If I am lucky, the glow is still around us, we are not so separate, not torn, still expansive, as we come back to our smaller selves.

One night, I tell him what I experience, and ask if it's the same for him. He smiles. He is enchanted by the idea of it, I can see, but he says no, for him it's just good sex. After that, I rarely feel the sacredness when we make love. I begin to hate him.

Tantra teaches that sex is one of the doorways into the sacred. When I tell a woman who practices yoga, she says that I've known Krishna in another life, and so recognized him. She doesn't think it's crazy at all. All around the world there are stories about these special love-making experiences with gods or spirit beings. I live on that edge between what is true, what is sacred and magical, and where madness begins.

Poetry for Breakfast

It began at breakfast with my mother and grandmother telling me nursery rhymes. *Old King Cole was a merry old soul, and a merry old soul was he.* I sang and recited, in love with the music, the shapes of words in my mouth, thrilled and terrified by the image of the little girl with the curl in the middle of her forehead, who *when she was good, was very very good, but when she was bad, she was horrid.* Like me, I thought.

By fourth grade, I was in love with Poe. Edgar Allan Poe. Even his name sounded dark. The stories were scary, but the language—*"the silken sad uncertain rustling of each purple curtain"*—was delicious. *"I was a child, and she was a child / in that kingdom by the sea / and we loved with a love / that was more than love / me and my Annabel Lee."* So magical, the sound, and the love between children, how did he know about that? One morning I surprised my father by sitting down and saying with quiet intensity, *"True!—nervous—very, very dreadfully nervous I had been and am; but why will you say that I am mad?"*

When I was twelve, two books appeared in the bathroom library, books my father was reading in night school—a slim volume of poems by T. S. Eliot and the complete works of Walt Whitman. It seems odd to me now that it was Eliot and not Whitman who made me aware that poetry could illuminate the most daily activities. I remember reading Eliot's "Preludes," which begins:

The winter evening settles down
With smell of steaks in passageways.
Six o'clock.

The burnt-out ends of smoky days.
And now a gusty shower wraps
The grimy scraps
Of withered leaves about your feet
And newspapers from vacant lots;
The showers beat
On broken blinds and chimney-pots,
And at the corner of the street
A lonely cab-horse steams and stamps.

And then the lighting of the lamps.

I had a paper-route at the time, and every evening I opened doors into back hallways and the smells of people's dinners cooking. I'd felt the wind and rain, the leaves blowing around my feet. The only horse we had in our neighborhood was the one that belonged to the union boss that we all had a chance to ride around the neighborhood bonfire on Halloween, and the lamps lit in our neighborhood were electric and came on all at once, but it didn't matter. Here were the details of everyday life—of my life—caught in a music more subtle than Poe's, one I wouldn't understand for years.

Still later, in eighth grade, I discovered the sonnets of Shakespeare. I remember first reading "Shall I Compare Thee to a Summer's Day" in study hall. The power of it moved me—very literally—out of my seat and into the hallway, me, the quiet, serious student, skipping out of study hall in an ecstatic trance. For me, it's not the little hairs standing up on the back of my neck. I must get up and walk around, open doors, stretch, breathe deeply, dance, leap, hug someone.

I walked through the hallways filled with, and elated by, the power and beauty of the poem that was so much bigger than its parts. I walked the halls until the end of that class period, as the fire subsided into a sure, warm ember. I spoke to no one about it. I suspected there was no one I could speak to about it.

You might think that I began writing at this point. I did not. I thought of myself as a reader, as a listener. These voices that came to me in books—across the centuries, from places as far away as Europe or as close as Providence, Rhode Island—I considered kindred spirits, ones who understood my heart before ever I was born, ones who loved the world with particular passion, the ones who could make magic with words. It never occurred to me that I could become part of that conversation.

Where I grew up people wrote grocery lists, left notes on the door, signed birthday cards, wrote down directions to a beach or party, shared recipe cards. They wrote estimates for plumbing or painting jobs, police reports, measurements and material requirements for making a dress. They did not write poems. They did not write books.

In love with the world as I was, with every bird, leaf, flower, insect, cloud, and river, I turned to science, which was broken up inexplicably into biology, the study of life—which left out the clouds, rivers, and mountains—and the earth sciences, where I could find the secrets of wind and weather, the secret passion of earth deep beneath her skin. For the stars I had to look to astronomy; for lightning, to physics.

At first it was all just description upon description. I loved it for the careful attention it paid to the world. I forgot the teacher who in first grade had said that water wasn't alive, and how I put on my boots and turned my back and my heart on her. If she didn't understand that water was alive, I couldn't believe anything she said. I wanted to pay that kind of attention to the world. I wanted to get up close and cherish every bit of it.

It was only later that I questioned a system that kills in order to study life, that divides the world into living and nonliving, and assigns a hierarchy of worth to the entire world, a system that negates spirit, that sees the world only in terms of its physical manifestation, a world without magic, in which mystery means simply a puzzle to be solved, rather than a numinous something to be experienced, the matrix in which we all live, the experience that the poets, at their best, invite us into, make us remember.

Cribbage

It's eleven-thirty. I light the fire under the kettle. One of us puts the teabags in the cup, takes out the sugar and milk. The other grabs the cards and cribbage board sitting on the counter next to the toaster oven. We head for the dining room across from the small kitchen. It's barely big enough for the heavy pine table and four chairs. Some nights there are peanut butter wafers, some nights Oreos. At holidays, pie or toll house cookies.

My son shuffles, offers me the cards. Cut 'em deep, you weep, he says. Cut 'em thin, you win. I cut half a dozen cards from the top, and he deals. We both search our hands for possibilities, the pairs, the fifteens, and hope for the double runs of sevens and eights, the three fives and a jack. I turn over the top card. Right jack for one.

I played cribbage with my father late nights when I was in high school. Now I play with my son. Four. Fourteen. And an ace is fifteen, two. We love the intricate scoring, the announcing of each move. I remember when I taught him, when he was just old enough to add, the pegs racing each other like little people around the board. This is the one my father made when he was in the service, with gun-metal pegs, each hole drilled precisely into the maple block, polished a deep amber.

We discuss our favorite *Star Trek* episodes. Which is best, "The Trouble with Tribbles" or "Amok Time"? "The Doomsday Machine" or "Mirror, Mirror"? He throws down a ten. Twenty-five, he says. Go. He takes his point.

Would you rather live in Rivendell or Lothlorien? We agree on Rivendell because of the mountains. Who would you like to hang out with, Chewy or Worf? We invent our own Far Side cartoons. I like the Sphinx in a paper grocery bag, pyramids in the background that he's drawn me, now on the refrigerator door. It reads, The Sphinx Has Found a New Home.

We don't talk about school. We don't talk about Pink Floyd or *Nightmare on Elm Street* or comic books. We don't talk about blue jeans with laddered gashes under back pockets. We don't talk about putting on clean clothes after a shower. We don't talk about anger or depression or his father asleep on the other side of the living room. We don't talk about friends dead from suicide, overdose, car accidents.

We talk about the best way to make chili. Whether meatballs should have one or two kinds of cheese. He tells me I'm getting good at making kibbee, and that his friend Joe likes my beef stew. We discuss mashing vs. dicing garlic. We discuss being a chef, directing movies, stop-time animation.

Sometimes we talk about girls who like him as friends. We talk about drugs. Speed kills—that button wasn't made up by the department of health. Anything that's a white crystal is too potent for the human body. Does that include sugar? he says. Yes. Yes, it does. We're in the home stretch. He's got first count.

We talk about birth control. We talk about *Dune*, that desert world of sandworms and blue spice. We talk about *Romeo and Juliet*. The ending is a rip-off, he says. We talk about the latest dungeon he is designing, and the monsters he's creating based on real earth creatures. It's like the angler fish, he tells me, it dangles bait for humans, but the bait looks like a small child crying. That's just evil, I say.

We talk about love. How to know when you're in or out of it. He tells me his dreams, his nightmares. We talk about the cats, the time we had three mother cats and nine kittens. We talk about how the dog babysat the kittens, picked each one gently from the edge of their box, not letting them escape while the mama cat was outside, then killed a mother rabbit and brought the babies home to us, put them carefully into our hands.

One night, flying ants from under the stone porch swarm into the kitchen and make their way into the dining room. We swat at them, then realize it's Friday the thirteenth, and start laughing wildly. We know they'll be gone as soon as they mate, that the queen will start a new colony, and that it won't be in our kitchen. But for now, we're in a Hitchcock movie.

We talk every night. For years. When he leaves home to get his own apartment, he comes back and stands at the end of the bed and talks. I get up, we put on the tea. He shuffles, hands me the cards. Cut 'em deep, you weep, he says.

Teaching Castaneda

Biology was my subject. I loved everything about it—the beauty of life, and its secrets. The tiny *"animalcules,"* now called bacteria, protists, algae—visible only under the microscope. The discoveries, the diseases, the theories, the questions.

During my senior year in high school, when I was studying human physiology with Sister Mary John, my mentor, she went to a conference for several days, and had me cover her sophomore classes while she was gone. I taught cell anatomy—the parts of simple, single-celled organisms, diagramming them effortlessly on the blackboard, fielding questions, explaining things as I went along.

I went to Clark University, where I planned to major in biology. I was excited that Clark had an electron microscope—not many schools did back then. With an electron microscope you could see viruses. I imagined research in microbiology, pathology, medicine, ecology, but I became distracted by all the other subjects—philosophy, psychology, geography in particular. I think I still wanted to know, not everything, but the BIG ANSWER, and looked to philosophy, science, and then psychology. Geography I just loved because I loved it—especially physical geography, the earth herself. I loved it purely, as I loved biology, and saw them together as one subject.

In fact, pretty soon all of my subjects seemed to be one subject. I wrote a nine-page philosophy paper for my Primate Social Behavior class instead of the two pages on the readings that were on the syllabus. The professor was very tolerant I think now, but he did say I had to focus on the course material next time. At the time I thought he was one more scientist who'd specialized too much. I failed to notice I'd lost the scientific method along the way, and my love of biology had been pushed aside.

I turned to philosophy. I really had the lingo down, I aced my classes, headed study groups . . . because this stuff was great. Until it all led to existentialism, a dead end, the only possibility a jump into mysticism, a jump I eagerly took. That's where Carlos Castaneda enters.

Sister Mary John seems excited to see me when I start my teaching residency, and clearly expects my practicum to be successful. I am wearing black stockings, a hippy skirt and peasant blouse with no bra, and lots of jewelry, very far from the black watch plaid skirt, navy blue blazer, knee socks and penny loafers, and no dangly earrings of my teenage years here. She looks me over, but she doesn't say anything.

In the classroom, I am again teaching about cells. Sister Mary John and I have discussed the curriculum I will be teaching. Easy stuff. The same old stuff. As I'm talking, it all begins to seem meaningless. It seems much more important to tell them about a book I've been reading, an alternative to western scientific ways of thinking.

Carlos Castaneda. I am fascinated, obsessed with his ideas—I know there's something valid there—and his stories about a Yaqui sorcerer, of his experiences of spirits and allies and dream-worlds and drugs that we'd later find out were all made up. This is important stuff—I have to tell them about it.

Sister Mary John leans against the window sill at the side of the room. She's no longer smiling. She crosses her arms across her chest. I can see she isn't thrilled with what I am saying. Oh, well, I'll explain it to her later. After class, she takes me aside, gently, and tells me that while it is interesting, it is not appropriate for the class. It is not the curriculum we talked about.

I don't remember what transpired—and this is a recurring thing, that I don't remember things I said or did during these periods—but apparently I didn't stop teaching Castaneda, or I argued with her, I don't know. But the residency ended. She, Sister Mary John, whom I'd loved and respected, threw me out.

It was her fault, of course. A narrow-minded nun, I told myself. But this was not some creationist. This was a 1960s ecumenical nun who was a scientist herself. She taught us about Darwin and evolution. She talked about how science and religion were both searches for truth, and that though sometimes they were at odds, as with Galileo, if something was true, it would last and the contradictions would disappear.

I don't know how long I was on the Castaneda binge, the first of many such binges. I was obsessive, strung-out, single-minded, intoxicated. I wanted to tell everyone, I wanted to convert them, and I was angry if they didn't get it. If they disagreed, or were skeptical, or if they just didn't want to hear me rattle on about it yet again, I became enraged, contemptuous. I yelled, cursed, destroyed them with my superior logic.

It took me three tries at practice teaching before I passed. How could this be? I always aced my classes—everything came easily to me. How could I have this trouble passing a teaching practicum? I didn't try teaching Castaneda again, but at my next residency I had to leave classes to visit the nurse with faintness, breathlessness, and hot flashes. The nurse said I should see a doctor for asthma. My face was flushed, I was light-headed, and my heart was pounding. Nobody suggested anxiety attacks.

Eventually I did my practice teaching in an English class, teaching poetry. It was a pleasure, a challenge, all the things teaching can be. But that first failure with Sister Mary John—what's odd to me is how I put it behind me, didn't think about it, forgot the details and blamed it on the fact that it was a religious high school. At no time did I look back and think, What the hell was I doing, teaching Castaneda to a high school biology class?

It was the 1970s—I had no one to tell me my behavior was bizarre, because who gets to define normal, anyway? Wasn't insanity just misunderstood in this culture? Didn't some cultures find wisdom, spiritual specialness in insanity? And those politicians, they're crazier than any of us.

Looking back, it is both surprising and not surprising that I had no inkling that I wasn't behaving normally, that my thinking was so strange. I hung out with druggies who were so much weirder than me, who dropped acid, had multiple sex partners, who lived and breathed Hendrix, ran a dope business out of the chem lab while pursuing double majors in their spare time. How could I tell what was real and true, and what was not?

I prided myself on not dropping acid or doing mescaline, on only smoking pot or hash, and occasionally a little opium. I wasn't going to put my baby in the oven on some acid trip. So see, I was one of the sane ones. Not like Michael, who stripped naked and went running manic through the park, or Steven, who took his own life and sent a letter to the school paper blaming us all. How the hell could I find normal in all this? The truth is I was afraid to drop acid, afraid I'd trip out into the Crazywoods and never come back.

I chose a mate who had his own craziness. Of course. We promised each other, after watching *One Flew Over the Cuckoo's Nest*, that no matter what, we'd never have each other committed. Surely we had some idea that insanity, madness, was a possibility. We even knew how it would go—me into mania, and him going slowly, quietly crazy.

We knew because we were already experiencing some of this process, we just couldn't make it any more conscious than the "what if . . ." scenario. Maybe others spoke similarly to each other, but I can't help thinking that somewhere, down deep, we knew how close we were, how little it would take to tip the balance, how very fragile we were.

Losing Them

One after another they fall out of my body, these babies I cannot hold onto. The first, just as I go back to school after a year-and-a-half maternity leave no one expected me to return from. All morning at school I bleed, until one trip to the bathroom leaves me empty. Empty, where I should be full. A friend walks me home. One fell out of me on Christmas Eve—the sudden cramping, clots in the toilet. One was lost as snow fell silently, another to howling dry winter winds.

Then there is the numbing pain, the diarrhea, the vomiting, the massive infection that could have been avoided if only the doctor didn't think my body should clean itself out naturally, that I didn't need the D&C that would have cleared my womb of the debris of pregnancy. The fever dreams, the visit to the doctor, the rush to the hospital where they push me through the halls on a gurney, where at every desk I hear nurses, technicians, interns, people with clipboards, with their hair covered, saying my name.

I don't know if I'll come out of this surgery. I tell my new husband to take care of my son. I am calm in my terror. I want to make sure my son will be all right. There is blood that is drawn, an intravenous line. They say count, and I do, 10, 9 . . . When I wake, everything looks far away and tiny. I am in isolation, quarantine. Everyone who comes in must put on gowns and masks. I will never have another child, they tell me. I am lucky to be alive.

It is not winter that I hate, not the time when they left my body, it is summer, when they should have been born. For years everyone is pregnant, the world is full of baby carriages and strollers. There is no ceremony, no acknowledgment of these ghost children, and I am torn in body and spirit.

It is years later when the doctors decide I have summer depression, a kind of reverse SAD, but it's not that. Outside, baby birds are chirping, tiny bunnies eat grass at twilight, ducks swim in formation behind their mothers. I hear the silence, where there should have been the cries of newborns.

Meditation—The Barren Road

I am sitting somewhere a foot above my body and I'm looking at the back of my head. I am following a road through a scorching desert, there is a sphinx, there is a question. The question is What is my face before my parents were born? I follow the question down the road and into a canyon. On the cliffs of the canyon there are the Screamers. They are here every time I walk this road. Their screeching drowns out everything. I am trying to find the answer—what was my face . . . no, this isn't it, no, no, and the Screamers are wailing now and I am breaking into a sweat.

I can see myself sitting in full lotus, I am dimly aware of the cushion I'm sitting on, that I'm facing a wall, but at the same time I am walking, following the question. The way is dry, the sand cliffs a grainy brown, and there is still shrieking coming from the ledges. I know I will die if I don't stop, I know they are not real, but if I don't stop this walking my heart will stop, already I can't breathe, I don't know, I don't know, what was my face before my parents were born?

If I do this every day, I will find the answer, I will become enlightened, there will be an end to pain. But every day I end up in the same place, walking this barren road, the Screamers on the cliffs above me.

The Taster

I am pouring a glass of cranberry juice. When it's full I'll take it out to the living room, where I'll ask my husband to taste it before I drink it.

It's botulism I'm afraid of. It can kill you in twenty-four hours. *Clostridium botulinum*. It's everywhere, it's a miracle more people don't die from it, but luckily it's anaerobic—it thrives in oxygen-free environments. It also doesn't survive high temperatures, so boiling will kill it. People get it mostly from home-canned vegetables, but last week, in Indiana, a family died from eating a can of mushrooms from the supermarket.

I remember eating mushrooms from the can when my mother made pizza on Sundays nights when I was a kid. Now it creeps me out. Now I only eat fresh mushrooms, which my mother is afraid of because they are, well, mushrooms.

I try to avoid food that comes in cans. No more tuna, no more baked beans, no more canned soups, peaches, pears, no more kernel corn. But I have to drink cranberry juice. I have to drink cranberry juice because I've been having UTIs and cranberry juice is antibacterial. I've considered boiling it first, but that might destroy whatever it is I'm drinking it for. My husband has to taste it before I'll drink it.

At first, I just invite him to have a glass of juice with me. But the truth is, he doesn't much like cranberry juice. Why do you want me to have juice when I don't want it? Finally I tell him. I'm afraid to drink it. Afraid of botulism. No amount of talk would make the fear go away.

I've drunk cranberry juice without having him drink some with me and here's what happens. As soon as I drink it, I start thinking, maybe this is the one batch that's got botulism in it. No one ever thought people would get botulism from those supermarket mushrooms, and they did, so maybe I'll get botulism from this cranberry juice. That's crazy, I tell myself. But I start checking for symptoms.

There's a scratching at the back of my throat. I feel itchy. Do my knuckles seem swollen? I start pacing, waiting to see what will happen. When should I call Emergency? And for what? There's no antidote.

It doesn't matter that people are not seeing my symptoms. They're not inside my body. What do they know? They say I am fine, but I am not fine. I'm waiting for the inevitable pain, the cramping muscles, the loss of breath. I'm going to die.

Really, I know there's no botulism in the cranberry juice. I wouldn't ask him to drink it if I thought it would kill him. No, I need him to drink it with me so when the panic comes, I can look at him and see he's not dying, because if he's not, I'm probably not either.

Horse Dream I

I am in a room with wooden floors and two windows with long, white sheer curtains. The curtains move with the light breeze. The room is bare except for a grand piano and a light grey dappled mare. The keyboard is not visible, the piano faces away from me, and the horse walks from behind it, in front of the windows. She looks at me sadly, with great tenderness. Then she turns and walks over to the door in the back wall, which opens. There is light coming from a stairwell. She looks at me over her shoulder, as if in farewell, and goes through the door and down a flight of stairs. I am desolate at her leaving. As I turn back to the room, I see the piano crashing silently to the floor.

Wretched

Tonight I'm wretched. I thought these meds were supposed to work, but I've been slipping into a depression, getting worse each day. I'm irritable and pessimistic during the day, but at night I'm really despairing. I keep thinking I might as well be dead. I'm not planning anything, but life seems useless. My life seems useless.

I used to sleep and sleep. Now instead of just being tired, I'm desperately sad. I am really afraid I am going into another one of those mixed manias or frantic depressions. I still have no sense of whether what I am thinking, what seems to make sense, comes from any real place, or just chemical soup. My unstable moods are not being controlled by these meds I agreed to take.

Sometimes I think we go crazy just so people will put us away somewhere and take care of us for a while. Just to not have to think, not have to answer to anything or anyone. My brain, my feelings are all on overload, and I can't get away. Like the T-shirt: wherever you go, there you are.

Sometimes when I feel sad, I see myself huddled in a corner, crying, but tonight I don't have that separation. I am here, completely, in my body.

People say things. They say, "You'll never be a bag lady." Or, "If you need anything, let us know." Or, "If we can help . . ." They don't mean it. It is just something they say. What do they mean, never be a bag lady? I am out of money. I've lost my home. They don't say, Come stay with me until you sort things out. Nobody says, Do you have groceries?

But that is not really true, I have to tell myself, it is only how I feel. It is depression talking. My sister does say, Come stay with me for a while. She takes me out to buy clothes, towels, pillows for my bed. My son and his wife take me into their home. My brother pays to have my piano moved and tuned. He helps me move out of my apartment and puts stuff into storage for me. My friend from high school shows up and takes me out to concerts, out to lunch and museums, and cabaret night at the Club Cafe. When my car dies, another brother gives me the old one sitting in his yard. There are a lot of people supporting me, but depression says otherwise, says I am totally alone, nobody cares.

I call friends. Some of them are worn out. Some of them drop out of my life. Everyone it seems, is scheduled. No one can impulsively have a cup of tea. I grew up in a world where you just showed up, just went over to someone's house and opened the door. Let me put the kettle on, they would say. Have you eaten?

Baby

He calls me Baby. Babe, he says. Baby. It's the Lovie name, the Honey-SweetieSugar name, the OldLadyMama name, the name he says over and over in the night. The name he says when he comes up behind me and puts his arms around me and I am surrounded by his warm smell and he talks low into my neck, growls into my hair. Babe, he says, Baby.

One night after a poetry reading, I hear my name and turn. It's him, talking about me to someone. I don't hear the rest of the sentence, just his voice saying my name. I've forgotten this pleasure, the sound of my name in my lover's mouth. I want to hear it again, I want that caress, that other intimacy, the one that calls me out from all the others.

At home, I tell him, you never call me by my name. I want you to. He tries. He says my name. But it's tentative. I feel shy. Touched in a different way. We make love. Baby, he says. Baby.

I wait for him to say it again, but he doesn't say it again. Each time, I have to ask him. Why won't you call me by my name? I love to hear you say my name. He's tried, he says, but he just can't. It doesn't come naturally. I feel like a beggar each time I ask, so I stop asking. Babe, he says. Baby.

Sunday Afternoon with Betty Grable

My mother is standing in front of the television, blocking the football game my father is trying to watch. It's Sunday afternoon, the dishes are washed and put away, my sister and I and both our husbands are sitting talking or watching the game. My mother stands in high heels, a tight aqua sweater, and silky white panties. She faces away from my father, legs together, hands on her hips, the TV light flashing behind her, looking over her shoulder like the Betty Grable pinup from World War II. Honey, she says, do you think my legs are getting fat? My father smirks, then says, your legs aren't getting fat, now let me watch the game. My mother shifts her weight from one foot to the other, smiles at him over her shoulder, and says, Are you sure, honey, are you sure they're not getting fat? They go back and forth like this for a while, until my mother is satisfied and leaves the room. We hear her in the kitchen, making coffee, cutting cake, talking in a soft, high voice, trilling to the canary in its cage over the sink. It is just another Sunday afternoon. We don't think anything of it, my mother in heels and underwear, a sweater girl, our husbands looking, or looking away.

Islands of Sanity: Poetry

Not everything is a symptom, although after diagnosis it may feel like it. Life goes on, fills in the cracks. Jobs, marriages, children, grandchildren. The places I am calm and healthy, the places I am not.

Writing is one of those places where I am not crazy, the madness of poetry is not the debilitating madness of bipolar. No matter what else is going on in my life, when I write, it's a process that brings me to clarity. I focus on the world. I write stories from my childhood, portraits, moments that have resonated throughout my life. I bear witness, I retell history and traditional stories. I describe the changing feathers of a goldfinch, the blessings of apple trees, the lake, the trees.

I get drunk on sound. I remember chants we said in church when I was a child, the "Blessed Bees" my sister and I called them, that began "Blessed Be God, Blessed Be His Holy Name, Blessed Be His Precious Blood, Blessed Be His Sacred Heart, Blessed Be Mary, the Mother of God." Now I write two-beat lines, I walk around speaking words aloud, each one repeating a sound from the last, I follow the melodic line of a prose poem. I count syllables, five seven five seven five. I cherish names: Innisfree, Quinsigamond, Trois Rivieres, Pemigewasset.

I learn to break lines by breath, for emphasis, for rhythm. I follow the spirit of the poem to discover its form, like a jazz musician taking a solo out and bringing it home to that satisfying, inevitable last line.

In my thirties I begin teaching in the Massachusetts Writer-in-the-Schools program. I invite students into the process. We become writers together for the weeks I am there. As I go from student to student, talking quietly about their writing, a teacher tells me she has never met anyone so patient. I'm surprised. I think about my nightly rages. When I was a child, my grandmother told me I had my mother's temper, a redhead's temper, even though I wasn't one. And it's true, I fall into rages I can't control.

But what the teacher says is also true. When I teach, I am calm. My attention is focused outside myself, on something bigger, on sharing this passion for language and vision. It is the same power I feel when the first words leave my mouth at a reading—no matter how nervous I may have felt beforehand, sweating, my gut cramping, agitated and unable to focus, when that first line is spoken, I am grounded, I am the voice through which the spirit of the story, the spirit of the poem speaks.

When I'm depressed, I don't write enough. When I'm manic, I write for days, weeks, carried in a flow of words, sounds, images—blessed, until I crash, empty, into another century of sleep.

The madness of poetry is something I court. When I was a young poet, we liked to say to each other, "I spent the weekend in bed with the Muse." Yes, come to me, seduce me, show me visions, make me mad with poetry.

My Bookstore

When I sit down at the breakfast table, I am revved by a new idea. I think I'm going to open a bookstore, I tell my daughter-in-law. I'm tired of all these corporate bookstores that have bought out all the indies, and there's no place to browse poetry or Native lit, or LGBTQ, or women's or multicultural, or really great kids' books.

Are you sure about this? she asks. It's a big thing, starting a business.

I love books and I love bookstores, and I know I can do this. We'll have poetry readings, music, storytelling for kids in the morning, and an evening storytelling program for adults. I am busy planning the menu for the café.

But you haven't gotten out of bed for three weeks, she says.

I brush it aside, it's all a thing of the past, and Marci worries all day. When Chris gets home, she tells him, Your mother wants to open a bookstore. She can't get out of bed for three weeks, and now she's working on a floor plan.

She's not going to open a bookstore, he says.

She's been talking about it all day. She's serious about this, Marci says. You should see how enthusiastic she is.

I know, he says. But don't worry about it. She'll forget about it by tomorrow. And I do.

The New House at Center Harbor

If I were there instead of here, would I be depressed? I am swinging low tonight, easily irritated, feeling as if everything is hopeless and that my plans for buying the house are pie-in-the-sky pipe dreams. How will I ever afford it? How can I believe that my life will be better, that I can create a new life of my own?

But that is tonight. I have gone over the numbers. I've looked all over Craigslist real estate sites to find rentals, and the prices are ridiculous. And a lot of places are just plain ugly. It's better to buy than to rent.

I know this house is not perfect. No place is. It's like a relationship. Is it perfect for me, right now? And I guess I think, yes, it is.

If I were there tonight, for one thing, it would be clean and neat. The food would be there because I bought it. My work spaces would be open to use whenever I want. I could play piano without bothering anyone, take a bath in the claw tub, listen to music that I choose, leave the sewing machine open and fabric swatches on the wall.

Every morning there would be light in my room, and outside–the lake and the mountains. I would be able to grow plants in my house again, outside these dreary dark rooms. I wonder how to set it up. Where I want the piano. Where I want my painting studio, the quilting table, the writing desk. Do I want my books out, or should I make the back bedroom a library?

I think I want the painting area in one of the two front rooms, by the windows looking out on the lake where there's lots of light. I can store finished work upstairs—but it's not on central heat, so I wouldn't want the paints there. Maybe the fabric and some books, and even the sewing machine if I'm not in the middle of a project.

The kitchen is small, the fridge is in a little closet pantry but I can't have everything right away, can I? And if it's only me, it should be okay. And there's a nice size dining room, where I'll probably end up doing a lot of writing and quilting and maybe gourds as well.

There's a little niche under the stairs where I'll put a small desk. Maybe there's room there for a printer and scanner, too. I don't want those to take up a lot of room; I want them tucked away so the front rooms can be without techno-clutter.

I love the front bay windows. I will spend a lot of time just looking out of them, even at night. I'm eager to see what the perennial garden looks like, what can be rescued from a few years' neglect, how I can make it mine. I will have a small veggie and herb garden out back. I'll make sure to have someone come and help me with that right away, the tilling, making the raised beds. It's a one-time expense if I do it right. I can grow my own gourds and dry them in the upstairs room under the roof.

There's an apartment upstairs that's rented, and the best part is a huge barn, with a heated work space where I could make assemblages, and what was a little summer antique store that would be perfect for selling crafts, books, and giving workshops. It's a short walk to the best fabric store in the Northeast.

The upstairs of the barn could be turned into another apartment— one for myself, with a good kitchen and a big front room looking out at the lake. If I did that, the rents from the other two apartments would pay the mortgage, and I think I could make a go of it with my artwork, workshops, and a good reading schedule.

If I can build a life for myself in this house, the boys, my grandsons, will have a place to visit, maybe stay in the summers. It will be a different kind of world than the techno world they live in most of the time. I want to take them all around Abenaki, the Dawnland. They need to know who they are, how they are connected to this place, those places of importance to our people. The world may change enough in their lifetimes that they will need that knowledge.

There are lots of artists in the Whites, I'll be walking into that community. And when I write, do art, the world smiles. I think there is work that I'm supposed to do, and the Grandmothers have shown me this place where I can do it, yet I'm afraid sometimes because I know my illness can put a glow on things. It makes it harder for me to trust. But I can see myself in this place, doing my work, having a big bear dog, a garden, space to heal. It looks over Winnipesaukee, but is in the village—I could walk to the market, the library, the quilt shop, the diner. There must be a theatre nearby.

I've done all the numbers, and if I can get the mortgage, I will have enough money to do it. I've been over it and over it and I'm sure I can do it.

The one thing I forget is that although I have saved up a down payment I have no income. No job. No bank will ever give me a mortgage. And I know I can't have a straight job, I can't be with people, I'm sleeping half the time and having panic attacks. I don't want to, but I have to let go of the house.

the trees
are
small
in the
crazywoods
and spindly
everything
is whispering
where
are the elms
where
are the chestnuts
what
is happening
to the
maples
what is
happening
to the
dogwood
the earth
burns
our feet

When You Can't Keep a Job

When you can't keep a job, when panic attacks send you to the restroom several times a day, when people spritzing their desks with Windex, or talking loud, or walking by enrage you, when someone moves your Kleenex box and you feel attacked, when you rearrange the entire accounts payable files according to some new system only you can see the merits of, when the lights hurt your eyes and you put on sunglasses, when you bang your fist on the time clock, when you throw off your apron during lunch rush and walk cursing through the restaurant on your way out the door, when you hesitate, when you forget your train of thought, when your students ask you if you're okay, when you know you're not okay, when you try to do your best, but cannot.

Denied

I hang up the phone. There's a long wail coming out of my mouth. I am at the desk upstairs at my brother's house where I've been staying temporarily until my disability is approved. I went to the hearing in December and now it's February, and I just got the call. Denied.

My head is in my hands as I lean on the desk. Then I am leaning back in the office chair, howling, my arms wrapped tight around my chest, holding myself together.

My sister-in-law comes upstairs. She thinks someone's died. And she's right. My life has been taken away. Where will I go, what will I do, what will I live on? I've been hanging on, waiting for this lifeline, but there will be no lifeline. I have applied too late, they say. My diagnosis came five months after the deadline. All those misdiagnoses are costing me my disability.

I leave and go to my son's for a few days. He calms me down. We can make a plan, he says. Things will turn around. When I return to my brother's, things are different. I have freaked my sister-in-law out. I can't stay here anymore, she says. She picks a fight. We say terrible things to each other. She tells me to pack and get the hell out. I'm upset because I don't have my meds. I don't have a doctor, and I can't get meds without a doctor. I'm afraid I will be out of control.

I drive around. I don't know what else to do. I need to find a doctor. This is an emergency. I go to the ER, where I sit and cry in the waiting room. A young man next to me says kindly, I'm so sorry, I'm so sorry. Things will get better. I don't know what he thinks has happened to me, maybe that someone has died. I'm such a wimp sitting here sobbing, but

I can't stop. I can't speak, so I just nod and nod at him and rock myself and finally someone calls my name.

I tell the woman right away that I'm bipolar, without my meds and terrified. I am still crying. Don't worry, she says, we'll get you your meds. I start to calm down. She asks for my name, and I tell her. She writes it down. Address? she asks. I don't know what to say. I look around the room as if there will be an answer somewhere. But it is all icy blue walls, wide empty counters, shelves of bandages, and boxes of rubber gloves.

Well, I say, I've been staying at my brother's but my sister-in-law just kicked me out, so I don't know what my address is. So, you're homeless, she says. I am. I'm homeless. I start sobbing again, nodding my head yes. Yes, I realize, I am homeless.

Five years later—it takes that long to get another hearing—another judge at another hearing will ask me what set me off, what exacerbated my illness, what happened to throw me into another episode. You don't want to hear it, I'll tell him. It was hearing that my disability was denied.

I move in with my sister, I move in with my son and his wife, everywhere is temporary. I have no home and I have no center. I swing wildly day by day, hour by hour. This whirlwind does not stop for years. I am thrown back. It's as if I've never taken meds, because now I take them and they're not working.

My son talks with a disability lawyer to get some clarification, to see if we can do anything. I can't be involved. I can't let myself hope again. I feel like rolling into a ball under the blanket. I feel like buying a shotgun. I understand for the first time the rage of people who do that—powerless, fucked over, with nothing left to lose.

Islands of Sanity: Grandsons

I keep the crazy times separate. They do not exist within this time with my grandsons. On other days, I may sleep, I may do Tarot spreads, I may shop wildly on the net or in bookstores, I may weep in the shower, but on Memere days, I am calm, I am grounded and reliable. I do not rage.

Joe is born, then three years later, Adam. I sing lullabies, stack blocks, heat up bottles. I change diapers with joy, talking, touching their toes to their heads, tickling their bellies. I watch them three days a week while my daughter-in-law works. She brings them over at noon, and my son picks them up at suppertime. Each night I make supper, with Joey watching from his bouncy, then from his high chair, then eventually he is on a chair next to me, helping me stir the batter for corn bread or pour the juice into a glass, and Adam is in the bouncy chair. When my son and husband come home, the boys are playing, dinner is ready, I am not raging, I am not sad, I am being Memere.

We go for walks. From the stroller Joe reaches out and touches the soft needles of the pine saplings. Baby pine trees, I tell him. Baby trees. Each time we take the path, he puts his hands out. Baby t'ees, he says. Later, we push the stroller together, and he teaches Adam how to brush the five-leaf bundles, how to avoid the prickly tips and slide down the long needles that bend gently against his hand.

One night I sit in the screened-in porch, Joe in my arms. It is a cricket night, the air warm and moist, full of the scent of pines and leaf mulch. Listen, I croon to him, Listen. We are together, surrounded by sweet singing in the dark.

I collect the ceramic animals from the Red Rose tea boxes, and line them on the window sill over the kitchen sink. At least one day a week, Adam stands on a chair and washes them all in the dishpan full of sudsy water. He rinses each one carefully and puts them on a folded dishtowel. He does this for me. Let me wash your animals, Memere, he says. Oh, they're so beautiful and clean, I tell him when he's done.

At the consignment shop, I buy a changing table. I buy a crib. I find a used carriage at a yard sale. A stroller. A walker. One day there is an amazing rocking horse painted like a carousel horse, in pinks and whites and silver. I take it home. Joe is three and rides on it all day. He stands on the saddle and does tricks. He is sure-footed, and I'm not anxious, and he never falls. When Adam gets old enough, he prefers to pet the horse, take care of it with his doctor set, rub it down with a rag. He wants to make sure the horse is happy, and brings it grass from the yard to eat.

Joe makes lines of Hot Wheels and firetrucks on the coffee table. Adam builds roads and towers. We all create landscapes with rocks and shells and pine cones and silk scarves. There are little people and animals, and stories in everything.

I sing "Tura Lura Lura" and "Down in the Valley." *Beautiful beautiful brown eyes, beautiful beautiful brown eyes, beautiful beautiful brown eyes, I love Adam's pretty brown eyes.* Then we sing *Beautiful beautiful green eyes* for Joe, and on through the family. *Had an old dog and his name was Blue, betcha five dollars he's a good dog, too. Ravioli, tasty ravioli . . . did you get it on your chin? Yes, I got it on my chin! On your chin? On my chin! Whoa!!!!!*

When Chris and Marci watch *American Idol,* I say, They should have a competition for grandparents. They look at me, shocked, as if I might mean it. No, they say, no.

Crazy Talk III

His specialty is ADD, so it is not surprising that before I'm in his office for ten minutes, he's diagnosed me with it. I don't know how, because he's barely said anything other than commenting on my weight, as in, you could lose a few pounds. Nevertheless, he prescribes a few drugs— one that keeps me in a stupor, one that makes me feel like snakes are crawling up my legs, and one blessed one that seems to calm me down.

Getting Fat on Antidepressants

It is the age of Prozac, so it's not surprising they put me on an antide-pressant. I gain twenty pounds, then twenty more. I'm hungry all the time. I don't sleep at night, but I take naps, sleep the days away. My mind is foggy and slow.

I'm still depressed, so they up the dosage. I eat and eat, but I am never satisfied. I try to read, but I forget what I've read and have to go back over things again and again. I forget entire books. I see the titles and know I've read them, *The Bonesetter's Daughter, A Plague of Doves, Jazz, The Liar's Club, The God of Small Things*. Why can I remember nothing? I argue with my husband about movies. I want to watch *Farewell, My Concubine*, but he says we've already watched it. I'm sure we haven't. We decide to agree that I may have slept through it.

I gain another twenty pounds, then another twenty. I've gone from a size ten to a size twenty-two. My doctors are hounding me, blaming me, putting me on diets. Before the meds, I kept Hershey's kisses in a jar on the kitchen counter. Every once in a while, I'd reach in and take one, pull the white ribbon, unwrap the silver, place it on my tongue, and bite gently, let the chocolate melt slowly on my tongue as I pressed the lid closed and put the tin back in its place. That's all I needed. It would keep me for days, just that little bit of chocolate.

I'd heard people on TV talk about eating a whole box of chocolates, the jokes about getting the munchies and eating all the Oreos in a package, about premenstrual ice cream binges, and I'd thought—who would do that? I loved food, loved finding new tastes, the intense pleasure in my mouth. But just a little would do. An *amuse-bouche*. After that first rush of flavor and texture, who needed more?

Now I eat and eat, but hardly enjoy any of it. Now it is all gobbling, stuffing, guzzling. If I fill the tin with chocolates, by the time the first one reaches my tongue I am unwrapping the second, then another and another until the tin is empty and I am full and bloated, but still hungry.

One day, driving home from lunch at an Italian restaurant where I've eaten my favorite ravioli and meatballs, I fall asleep at the wheel and find myself in a ditch by the side of the road. I know I'm not sleeping well. I've got to get to bed earlier, I think. But when I try, I just lie there, my eyes wide open, until finally I get up and make my way to the kitchen where I make toast and jam and hot milk and finally go to bed and sleep. A few days later, it happens again. I wake up and swerve in time to miss a tree. This time I'm scared.

The doctor does tests. I have diabetes, she says. It's because I'm obese, I've let myself get fat and now I'm paying the price. She puts me on a diet. I try to stay on it, but I can't. I'm hungry all the time. I want carbs and I want them now, and I want them later. I keep the cabinets full of pasta, potatoes, chips, cookies, rice. I drink juice. It's healthy, at least a quart a day. I keep gallons in the coat closet. I'm a foodaholic, the doctor tells me. I should go to a group. But I know I'm really hungry. I'm hungry all the time.

I'm depressed. I'm depressed even though I'm taking the SSRI every day as directed. It does nothing for my depression. In fact, I learn later, SSRIs don't help people with manic-depressive illness, they can throw us into mania. I keep taking it because I'm too depressed to think of going off it. Still, even after I begin taking a mood stabilizer that almost immediately makes me feel better, I stay on the SSRI. No doctor ever suggests I should come off it. They just keep prescribing it, and I keep taking it—like a good girl. I am being compliant. I am trying to get well.

Here is what they don't tell you. SSRIs like Prozac, like Cylexa and Lexapro, the drugs I was taking, increase insulin resistance. Increased insulin resistance is what leads to type II diabetes. On the internet site for the drug I'm taking I find a warning embedded somewhere among the side effects that the insulin resistance caused by the drug can "push people into diabetes."

I remember an article someone wrote on depression. He'd gone to a depression support group, and what he noticed was that everyone there was overweight. We all know that. We all know "moderate weight gain" is a side effect. But no one explains why.

After twelve years, with eighty pounds of added weight, after my internet sleuthing, I finally get up the courage to tell my doctor, I don't think I need the SSRI. In fact, I say, I think it's never done anything for my depression. I tell him I have type II diabetes and the drug is making it worse. I mention insulin resistance. Yes, he says that can be a problem. He knew this all along. All the doctors know this.

I no longer have a full-length mirror in the house, I no longer have a scale. I have thrown away all my favorite clothes. I can't buy boots because my calves are too thick. In spite of my constant binging, it is as if I'm not eating at all. The carbs go directly to fat. I am, in fact, starving in a fat body.

When I look at photos of myself at fifty, I see a healthy-looking woman pushing her grandson on a swing. She is of average size. She has a waist. Her breasts are full and distinct from the rest of her torso. Her eyes are bright, her hair loose and wild. In a photo of me at fifty-five, I am standing next to a quilt at an opening of an art exhibit in which I have several pieces. What I see is a woman who looks sick. Her face is puffy, her body swollen. The tan suede vest with rose embroidery is stretched across her chest and stomach. It is not just the fat. There is illness here. Her face is red. She looks as if it's hard for her to breathe. She looks exhausted. Her hair looks as if it hasn't been washed.

We cut the dosage in half, then in half again. It takes four months before I am totally free of the drug. I am finally able to eat well, to take care of myself. The binges stop. I choose a low-carb diet to control my diabetes, and in a year my blood sugar drops drastically, almost back to normal levels. In a year's time I lose almost forty pounds, half the weight I gained while on the SSRI.

Here's what I would like to tell you: *The tin in my kitchen is filled with Hershey kisses. Every few days I take one out and eat it, savor the sweet complex flavor of chocolate. I am totally satisfied. I close the tin and put it back on the shelf.* But it's not that way. Insulin resistance is progressive. The cravings come back. This can't be undone.

To Whom It May Concern:

I am writing to request housing assistance. I am sixty years old, disabled with rapid-cycling bipolar illness, and destitute. In the past year, I've been divorced. My ex-husband has been unemployed for two years, and our home has been foreclosed upon. We went through our entire savings. I now have no money coming in and no home.

I have lived in five different places in the past year, including an apartment that I lost because I ran out of money. The other places were all temporary, with relatives. I am currently living with my son and his family, sharing a bed with my youngest grandson. It is very crowded, and though they have been very helpful, they have told me it must be temporary. It's putting a strain on their marriage.

It is also difficult for me to maintain stability here, since it's noisy, I don't have any of my things—I'm basically living out of a suitcase—and, as I said before, this is temporary.

All of the change has been extremely stressful, and hard on my illness. I need stability in my living situation in order to build stability in terms of my bipolar illness.

I have an application pending with SSI and also with SSDI. It is difficult for me to ask for help, but I am forced by circumstances to do so. Thank you for your attention and anything you can do.

Memere Stories: Sing á Memere

My husband comes home and finds me on my knees, sorting blocks and tiny cars into their bins. I enjoy putting the toys away—creating a tableau for tomorrow morning the way my mother did on Christmas day, all the toys and books displayed and full of possibilities.

When I'm done, I sit on the sofa. I'm tired, but it's a good tired and my heart is full. I say to him, surprising myself, Today is a day of perfect happiness. And so it is. These days come often during this time of caring for my grandsons—not only moments of joy, but of knowing and appreciating my own happiness.

Everything they do fills me with gladness. My daughter-in-law, exasperated, puts the crying baby into my arms. He is just two months old—she is still exhausted from the pregnancy and birth, and, I think, a little depressed. I wrap the blanket tight around him, put him to my shoulder, my cheek against his head.

Sing á Memere, I croon to him. Sing á Memere, *uh-n-uh* That's right. My daughter-in-law looks at me, surprised. Then her whole body relaxes as she sits in the armchair and closes her eyes.

Sunday Dinners

It's Sunday, I'm at my mother's house, and my brothers are plotting how to get a rise out of me. My sister is mashing potatoes, I'm stirring butter into the squash, and my mother is making gravy. The children are in and out of the kitchen, stealing a green bean, sticking a finger in the whipped cream of the chocolate pie my mother's made for dessert. There is a fist clenched inside me as there is every Sunday while I wait to make the inevitable mistake. I am a Catholic girl who got pregnant before I was married, then I got a divorce, and now I've married a social-ist Jew and my mother will never complain and she will never forget. Words fly out of her mouth like toads whenever I let my guard down. She has already told me that I'm atheist because my husband is, and that my family is hardly what you'd call a family, but I am here because it is Sunday and it is dinnertime, and now we sit at the table and my father says grace and we all eat. My brothers will say *uppity women*, or *the Pope said homosexuals*, or *abortionists should*, or *if they were Black they would've*. They have already decided on the bait. I will fall into their trap over and over again. I will think that if I just explain it right, but I can never explain it right because I am boiling over, scalding myself and everyone close by. They don't know and I don't know it is an illness, but if they did, would it make any difference?

Pookie

There is a dog in the yard across the street, on a leash and crying. It's raining and he's miserable. He's sitting on the grassy hillside in front of the house where there's no one home. How could they leave him like this? I want to help but he is not my dog, I should mind my own business, but after I've taken in the groceries and go out to close the trunk of the car he is still crying, and I can't stand it. I go over and unleash him and he starts dancing around me. We walk around to the back door and into the cellar where I rub him down with a big towel, and tell him it's all right, he'll be warm and safe here. He sits patiently while I rub him dry, his head slightly raised to let me dry his neck and chest.

He is a big dog, black, a Newfie mix, and when I lay a rug for him in front of the washer and dryer, he circles and lies down on it with a big sigh. I leave him there to go put the groceries away, and he does not whine, but puts his head down on his paws as if to wait or sleep.

When he's dry, I let him upstairs, and he spends the rest of the afternoon keeping me company as I knit, play piano, and read. When I see the lights go on in the house across the street, I let him out, and walk with him up the long stairs and ring the bell. I introduce myself to this neighbor I've never met, and tell her the story of the day, and how I took Pookie off his leash and into my cellar. She is grateful, it turns out—I'd been afraid she'd be upset, that Pookie was, in her mind, property. Instead she tells me she hates leaving him outside, but inside is worse, and that she worried about him all afternoon because he hates the rain. She tells me to take him any time, he'll love the company.

And so it begins. It's summer, and every day after breakfast I go outside and let Pookie off his leash. We spend the day together, mostly outside. I'm recuperating from a long illness, and I spend a lot of time sitting in a lawn chair reading and knitting, and he is content with this. One day I throw a ball for him, and he dutifully retrieves it and drops it at my feet. When I throw it the second time, he looks up at me and sits, as if to say, Didn't I just get that for you? And this is the way he is. He doesn't obey, he considers any suggestion of mine and then does what he thinks is right. He is a gentleman, and always waits for me to go through doorways first, walks in front of me without a leash, and waits at the corner of the streets when I say, Pookie, wait. He always sits when asked, lies down, and stays most of the time. But he is smart in that Newfie way that people sometimes interpret as slow-witted. He is not slow, he is considering.

Newfs have been our dogs for thousands of years. Their bones have been found in two-thousand-year-old digs and were described as "Indian bear dogs," so they were fully themselves already at that time. They were not pets. They were family members whose job it was to help carry household goods from one encampment to another. They tended children and elders and were expected to know when there was real danger, and to take whatever action was needed.

One evening, the neighbor comes over after work. I have a proposition for you, she says. She's in the service and has to go to Biloxi for training. She'll be gone six months, would I watch Pookie for her? I consider, then shake my head. No, I say. I think it would be confusing to him. But I will take him permanently if he wants to live here. She agrees. Pookie looks back and forth at us as we speak, these humans who've finally figured it out. That would be best for him, she agrees. She assures me before she leaves that he won't be any trouble. He rarely comes into the house anymore, she says. After she leaves, Pookie and I look at each other, then I get up and open the door, and we walk inside.

He has never spent the night with us before, and the first time there's a thunderstorm, I wake when he suddenly leaps onto the bed between us, shivering in fear. Nothing I do convinces him to get off the bed until I get up and walk into the other room with him, sit down and reassure him with scratches to his chest and behind his ears. He hates the thunderclaps and I think how loud they must be to him. I sit at the piano, then, and begin to play, and he lies down next to me, calmed by the familiar sounds. Storms should not be endured alone.

Our house has a walk-out basement, with sliding doors out to the back yard and huge windows, and we've finished part of it into a large room that houses the TV, a couple of sofas, my desk, and a table for sewing and other crafts. One afternoon, the sky darkens into a sickly green and the wind picks up and begins to wail and I remember tornado. We don't get them often here, but I still remember the legendary '53 tornado, when I was only three years old, and the color of the sky. Pookie begins to tremble, and I lead him to the three-foot thick doorway between the main cellar and the finished room which forms the perfect cave for the both of us. The storm passes, a small tornado touched down ten miles away and I understand finally that what Pookie needs during storms is that safe cave of his ancestors, the wolves.

Pookie spends most of the winter sitting on top of the snow we've piled high on the sides of walks and the driveway. During one huge blizzard that lasts for days and has us huddling in the living room around the wood stove after the power goes out, we call Pookie in, over and over again, but it's too hot for him inside, and within half an hour, he wants to be outside again, where the action is, happy in the drifting snow.

Giant dogs have short lives, and in this century of cancer, Newfs are particularly susceptible. After surviving an accident with a car that broke his hind leg, he develops a growth where the break had been. It's aggressive, spreads quickly to his lungs. The vet says it won't be long, and within a week of diagnosis, we take him back to the vet and sing him to sleep.

Our stories say that when we take the Star Road we eventually come to an abyss. The bridge that crosses it is held up by the dogs we've loved and who've loved us. My grandsons, who've never had a dog, say that cats are included now, that our cats help hold up the bridge. I hope that story is true, that Pookie will come from wherever he is playing or sleeping or working or thinking deep thoughts, to the bridge when I arrive walking from the other side.

Peach Cobbler

The problem with the peach cobbler began with the peach pie. I made my first peach pie from an old recipe that my friend's aunt gave her. I wanted a pie that I'd share with my girlfriends on a Friday women's storytelling night, and I decided this was the one. It was rich with cinnamon and brown sugar, fresh peaches and a crust flaky and full of butter. We'd all gone back for seconds.

That next morning the phone rang early. It was my brother, calling from New Hampshire, from Back Lake up near the Canadian border, where he, my father, and three other brothers, friends, and extended family had gone fishing.

Cheryl, he said, Dad died during the night. His voice was toneless, and so low I could hardly hear it. I found him in his chair this morning, he said. I thought he'd gotten up early to look out at the water, like he likes to do. I heard someone in the room wailing. It took a while before I realized it was me.

After that, the smell of cooked peaches brought only terrible sadness. I could still eat a fresh peach, but I couldn't bear to make peach pie, or anything that smelled of brown sugar, cinnamon, cooked peaches. The thought of it, the smell, the taste, all brought me back to that moment of the phone call, and the four of us eating pie and laughing the evening before my father took his last breath.

Now, my husband and I have moved to a new place. After unpacking and setting up the kitchen, I invite my husband's family over for dinner. That afternoon, he comes back from shopping with a bag full of ripe peaches from the local farm.

I look at the peaches, smell them, feel their ripe softness in my hands, and say to myself, It's time. I will make, not a peach pie, but a peach cobbler. I boil water, pour it into a glass bowl, drop the peaches in, one by one, and let them sit for a minute or two, then rub off their skins. I cut them up into a buttered baking dish and drop the biscuit mixture on top. Just before we sit down to eat supper, I take the cobbler out of the oven.

The table is set with new brightly-striped cotton napkins. My mother-in-law says they're too nice to use and folds hers neatly next to her plate. My sister- and brother-in-law follow her lead, fold their napkins, and set them aside. The dinner is pleasant—roast chicken, new potatoes, green beans from the local farm stand. We clean up the table, and set out dessert plates, cups for the coffee and tea. Then I bring in the peach cobbler.

The topping is lightly brown, the smells of cinnamon and brown sugar fill the room. And the beautiful sliced peaches, like golden summer light, fill the bowls, each topped with whipped cream. I eat with no sense of sadness. Conversation stops. Just the easy camaraderie of eating something homemade with people you love.

The next morning the phone rings. It's my sister this time, telling me that Bob, my mother's husband, has died of a massive heart attack during the night. I can't speak. Bob had just made us a huge mac-and-cheese casserole a couple of days before, after we'd been packing all day and gone to my mother's house to sleep over before the movers came in the morning. And now he's gone.

As I take my shower and get dressed, and drive the two hours to my mother's house, I can't get the peaches out of my mind. I baked a peach dessert twice in my life, both times followed by deaths. And not just any deaths, but my father, and then my mother's second husband. Even after fifteen years of being what had seemed overly cautious, there was something about me baking peach desserts that was too close to inadvertent witchcraft. Is there such a thing? Can you curse someone without knowing it? At night I dream a cauldron of peaches.

I can't talk about this to anyone, of course. I feel guilty. But there was no bad intention. I didn't know peaches, in my hands, had this much power. I try to tell myself this is just a coincidence, but deep in my heart,

I know different. There is something, some synchronicity, some witchery that connected my baking peaches with the death of men in my family. Peach cobbler. Peach Pie. Delicious. Deadly.

Years later, someone suggests making a cobbler with the fresh peaches they've brought with them from an orchard on the way to my mother's. Not me, I say, I don't make peach cobblers anymore. They look at me quizzically. I've only baked with peaches twice in my life, I say. And tell them the story. I am not surprised when my mother looks at me, horrified, and leaves the room.

Falling in Love with Diane

All my life I've been falling in love with women, but this time it's different—she loves me back. Even though I am in love with her, even though sex with him has become a rare thing, even though I don't trust him or respect him, I can't believe I can live on my own. I believe the lie he has taught me: that I'm totally dependent on him, that I'm too sick to take care of myself, to do anything for myself; that no one else would ever love me, and that he, in fact, does love me.

He brings me a cup of tea every night to prove this. At first I find this endearing—no one has ever done that for me, and I hold onto this as evidence that our marriage is still working in spite of his compulsive lying, his refusal to vacuum or wash the kitchen floor, things I can't do because of illness, that instead he does the dishes and laundry, things I can do easily. The kitchen floor becomes sticky, and I ask him over and over to wash it, but he won't. In therapy, the counsellor tells me I should outwait his stubbornness. How long should I wait? I ask him. Do you think ten months is long enough? He looks at my husband. Do you love her? Yes. Then why do you do this?

She is all in black. Her hair is inky, her eyes lined with black, her long nails deep red. She wears a long black skirt, wrap sweater, and chunky heels. She is a Gen X, she tells me. She is not political. Everyone is political, I say.

In class we are playing Good Indian/Bad Indian. I am questioning every text, challenging every reading; she just wants to get on with the class. This will change. She will learn the difference between heritage and identity. She will come out. She will decide not to finish her dissertation and any hopes of a prestigious job in favor of teaching at a junior college in her home town, teaching poor kids, working class kids. She will be the advisor to the LGBTQ group on campus. But for now, she believes the lie about her generation: they are not political.

He has gone through all our son's college money and spent it on—who knows? He doesn't leave tracks. He loses a job, gets a big severance package, and refuses to look for a job until all the money is gone and we are in debt.

She comes for an overnight visit. I'm sitting in the living room, reading, when she sits down on the sofa opposite me and plunks a huge tackle box on the coffee table. I didn't know she was into fishing. Will she want me to fish with her? Can I just bring a book and binoculars?

When she opens the tackle box, I think at first it is full of flies, feathers, and hooks, but the colorful lures are tubes of lipstick, bottles of nail polish, brushes. The light gleams on miniature scissors, clippers, and eyelash curlers.

She invites me to her apartment. I expect more black, skulls, posters of metal bands, but her place is all light colors, the smell of dinner cooking, a homey afghan on the couch. Everything is spotless. There is no clutter, even with her love of books. Her spices are on a lazy Susan on the counter that she twirls as she chooses for the dish she's making. She's invited me into her inner world, shown me the woman behind the Goth mask. Her intelligence, her brash voice, her irreverent sense of humor, the toughness she presents to the world, I know this—I did this—it makes me appreciate her softness and vulnerability even more. It is when I begin to love her.

I sing to her as she cooks, *I don't care if you're married, I still love you honey, I'll get you yet,* but it's me who's married and I want to tell her it doesn't matter. And so it begins, this friendship, the years of desire, sharing a house, cooking an Indian dinner and making so much pear chutney, we give jars to all our friends, drinking strawberry and champagne smoothies during a four-day blizzard, cuddling under covers in the unheated bed-room, but not lovers, not yet.

He says I can't make it on my own, and it's true that it's impossible for me to keep a job. The pain from fibromyalgia has kept me from working full-time since it hit me in my thirties. And, of course, there was the undiagnosed mental illness. Nevertheless, I go through periods of intense work, teaching in the poets-in-the-schools program, teaching adjunct courses at several colleges, writing, founding a woman's storytelling group with concerts over the fall, winter, and spring seasons, and in the schools. Now I'm in graduate school, in a PhD program I find unwelcoming and hostile to the Native critiques I write on the literature. My second book of poetry has just come out, and I'm doing readings several times a week on top of teaching, studying, and writing. I'm exhausted, it's too much, and the worst is the poisonous conflict. I cry from exhaustion and sleep for days.

When she tells me she loves me, I don't believe her. I want this, but I don't. I don't say what I should and she thinks I don't love her, but I do, I will love her for years, after I leave my husband for her, and go back to him, after she marries another woman, maybe forever, but for now, nothing is clear, no path seems possible.

She won't come to New Mexico with me because she doesn't want to disrupt her children's lives. I understand this. What I don't understand is how I end up living with my husband in an apartment on the west side of Albuquerque next to the frozen lava flows. Every day I come home from teaching under the famous big sky to a house grey with despair. The marriage ends but it doesn't end, until more lies propel me across country in a van full of clothes, books, papers, and fabric, a sewing machine gummed up by the swirling sand.

Divorce. I've already done it once. Twice—how would my family take that? And didn't I say never again? She says she doesn't want to be responsible for breaking up a family. She tells me she's sick of women.

She wants to watch the men play hockey. She tells me I'm not really a lesbian because I don't date other women. I don't want other women, I say, I only want you. For years we play this dance of desire, this come here/go away tango, until one day she invites me to lunch and I meet the woman she is going to marry.

Maybe this would have happened anyway. Love is never easy. I feed the birds in winter, they are my joy, they have gotten me through winters of illness, got me out of my bed and into deep snow to keep the feeders full of seed. She hates birds, she tells me. They shit all over the car. They squawk. They are good for nothing. She is aggressive in her dislike, and I don't understand until she tells me one day that her mother feeds the birds. Her mother, the one who sees the devil coming out of the television. I am not your mother, I tell her.

It's not clear, not even from this distance. I remember weeks of depression and days of overwhelming desire. She is my sister, my friend, my lover. She is smart, irreverent, funny. I only want to have her in my arms.

I loved her from within the cage of illness, from within that place where love as desire and love as action aren't integrated. How could I truly love someone when I couldn't see or feel anything but turbulence and confusion? How could I help hurting her and hurting myself? There was no diagnosis, there was no self-knowledge.

It takes a trip to the Dodge poetry festival, where she is too cold and I am stifling with the first hot flashes of menopause; an overnight in a Victorian bed and breakfast where I sing a Yeats poem to her in the dark, circling her palm with my fingers, and touching her breasts for the first time; and then finally a night we plan together, a claw tub, and she, finally, the girl in my arms. We are raucous lovers, we must be, because in the morning the landlady says she heard us laughing "into the wee hours" and comments on how good it is to have those girls' nights away. We laugh again and our eyes meet over the coffee, the bacon, the maple syrup.

Talk Doc: Julie

Although I've seen numerous therapists, Julie is my first Talk Doc, the first therapist I connect with, the first to help me make sense of this world I've awoken to, who helps me see that I am not bipolar, that bipolar illness is something I have, a disease that can be, if not cured, at least managed. She's a lesbian, so she'll never tell me my friendships with women are too intense.

One day I tell her that I feel sometimes like I'm trembling deep inside even though you can't see it from outside.

But you can see it, she says. You're trembling now.

Grand Poobah

In New Mexico, Carol tells me, We take care of our medicine people. They have gifts, but they can't take care of themselves, so we do it for them. She is talking about her brother. He is a Two Spirit, he has been married to two bishops and a movie star. And now a woman has given him a son.

He is charismatic. He is Coyote, a conman. He is a torch singer. He can call you with his thoughts. He is your best friend and your worst enemy.

in spring
puddles and pools
fill these woods
orange salamanders
crawl in the dark
following water

I follow
water
those creative
bursts
that episodic
joy
the world
full
of exuberant
meaning
those moments when
I remember
the world
with my old
eyes

Land of Enchantment I

The Sandias turned their watermelon-pink at sunset the last night of my first visit to New Mexico. I was there for a meeting of Native writers. It was May, and everyone was waiting for what they called "The Monsoon," which would bring rain every afternoon, they told me.

Not my idea of a monsoon. In the Northeast, we get thunderstorms pretty much every day of sunshine during the summer. And on the other days, well, mostly, it rains. I thought of monsoons as a southeast Asian thing—weeks and weeks and weeks of unremitting rain, but here in Albuquerque, the same weather patterns bring this mini-monsoon, one the desert, and everyone who lives there, waits for.

That last afternoon before I left for home, I thought it had arrived. The air darkened, a wind came up, the sky was working itself up to a good thunderstorm. And then the sky opened . . . and spit. That's what we would call it at home. Just a little spit of rain. I didn't know yet, the huge thunderstorms that would drop water that had nowhere to go except the arroyos, eroded ditches to my Eastern eyes, that filled with roiling water that swept away dogs and cars and cattle and children.

The heat pressed on my skin in an entirely different way in New Mexico than at home, where it was always a wet hand, a sweaty heat. If it gets over 80 degrees, we're in soup, and once it gets over 90, we're deep in chowder. There's no break in the evening—that water-drenched air holds the heat and smothers us without relief. We just have to wait for a break in the weather, for some Canadian air to blow our way. People in the West have trouble imagining this damp forest heat. It's only 85 degrees, they say, not 105. Now that's really hot. And it was. Just different. And those cool desert nights without mosquitoes give relief every single night.

This visit was a chance to see the place, to see if I might accept a job at UNM. The idea was that I would teach in the Native American Studies department and work on my dissertation. I wanted ultimately to teach back home, but there was this weird, unspoken requirement that you spend time away somewhere before anyone would hire you at home.

We strolled Old Town, and ate New Mexican chili, which came, I found out, in two colors, red and green, and had nothing to do with the Tex-Mex chili I knew, which was dismissed with contempt. We ate *posole* and *sopapillas,* which I thought of as New Mexican *beignets,* and great rounds of frybread, with butter and sugar, greasy and delicious, or covered with chili, Indian tacos. I was excited, enchanted, accepted the job, and in two months' time, had moved to Albuquerque.

Two days there, and I started getting up around 5:30 in the morning and taking a nap in the afternoon. This wasn't something I thought about, it was just my body's knowing, adjusting itself to place. I learned gradually to walk more slowly in the heat, to let my lungs adjust to the high desert.

The land, my eyes, that was something else. It took months before I could see anything but brown. Everything looked like a vacant lot back home, with the topsoil gone, and plants struggling to grow, with big stretches of gravel between them; not the natural lush growth, plants tumbling over each other, every square inch covered with green, where the streets and buildings are taken so easily back into the land if given a few years without human intervention. But then I noticed the sunflowers. Everywhere, in every yard, it seemed, Sunflowers. Some big ones, but mostly bushes sprinkled with small blossoms. And Roses! Who knew Roses liked the desert? They proliferated without any mildew, with very little care it seemed. On the other hand, the landlord left a note to remind me to water the tree outside every day.

Water a tree? Really? The only trees I ever watered were saplings on the day they were transplanted, and Christmas trees when we put them up in the living room. I felt sorry for this ornamental tree, not from this place, as much a stranger as myself, as hungry for water as I was. Every morning, before I showered, I took out the hose and gave the tree a good, long drink.

Stories and Storms

Give a person a few objects, give them a place, an event, or a few characters, and they will see connections, uncover meaning, make a story.

When I was a girl, at the first sound of thunder, my maternal grandmother went from room to room, blessing each doorway with holy water, then setting a small saucer of it outside the front door. She closed the curtains and gathered us around her, holding the baby as she rocked and sang to all of us, talking about the angels washing the floors upstairs, about bowling alleys in heaven.

My father preferred to watch storms up close. He pulled open the curtains and raised the blinds so we wouldn't miss any zigzag lightning or the size of hail stones that might fall. Storms were to be cheered on, like a sports team when they did something well. That was a good one, he'd say of a particularly strong lightning burst or a sudden clap of thunder. Way to go.

When I said, Thunder is scary, he told me, It's the lightning that can hurt you. So if you see the lightning it's already missed you. Thunder is just reminding you that you're safe. Every bright light, every crack and boom. One time we watched ball lightning land on the top of a telephone pole on the far edge of the field. It landed on top, rolled down the side, and, just before hitting the ground, exploded into sparks that disappeared into the humid air.

After my father built a wide concrete front porch, we watched storms roll in from the west. Under the protection of the overhanging roof, surrounded by the wet air, the rain splashing around us, we were part of the storm, the wind, the invigorating smell.

Watching a storm inevitably brought up memories of former storms, like the memories of baseball games or fishing trips, or the births of children. We told each other stories of storms we'd witnessed together, the ball lightning storm, the fallen birches, the cloud-to-cloud lightning, mighty voices of thunder. We told each other about the flooding of the front yard, wading through the cool water, the grass tickling our ankles, and how an hour later it was gone, absorbed into the underground rivers and lakes Dad told us about.

Together we remembered the time the eye of a hurricane passed right over us and we went outside into twenty minutes of blue sky, and how the winds raged afterwards around that peaceful center. My father told about the fierce tornado of '53 that started out in the Quabbin, twenty-six miles west, and traveled for forty-seven minutes on the ground and left a swath half a mile wide here in Massachusetts, where we hardly ever had tornadoes. What I remembered was my grandmother holding tight to my hands, hurrying us home from St. Anne's church, the green sky, hailstones we collected in buckets, and then going to see the houses and trees knocked down the next day just a few streets from our house.

When I was in eighth grade a storm came up during baseball practice and a boy at my school ran toward the building carrying one of the bases over his head for protection from the rain. Its metal clasp drew the lightning, and killed him instantly. His story became one of many cautionary tales. Don't stand under a tree. Carry nothing metal. Be the lowest thing around, under a canoe or rowboat or a bulkhead, or if worse came to worse, lying in a ditch or in the tall grass.

The stories about angels and bowling alleys were fun, but truth was on the front porch. The storms gave us rain and wind and the good deep breaths we took of charged air. We gave back our attention, our applause, our stories.

New York in Albuquerque

I find a coffee shop just across the river in Albuquerque that has lox-and-cream-cheese bagels. I am ecstatic! How did this New York delicacy find its way here amidst all these chilis and over-spiced food? It is an oasis.

When I go there with a student at night, I find it full of women. It's a lesbian hangout. And I only went there for breakfast! There is a woman who's eyeing me, and I smile back. This is possible, this Albuquerque.

A few days later, I am with my husband at lunch, eating my bagel with lox, cream cheese, onion, and tomato. The same woman is there. She raises her eyes and smiles and I smile back, over my husband's head, bent over his roast beef sandwich.

Why do I stay in this marriage? I am so afraid no one will love me.

Leaving

In my journals I keep finding these words: I have to leave this marriage. Over the course of two decades, these words are written, each time like a new revelation. I must leave this marriage.

Each time I'd written the words, I'd come to some kind of clarity. In some window between mania and depression, I found my way each time to this truth: I must leave the marriage.

But each time, depression closed over me, created a dense fog between me and the world. Years went by. Decades. Only from time to time could I make my way through the fog to that truth: I must leave this marriage.

Six months after I start taking meds, I leave the marriage. Everything I have feared happens. I lose my home, I am destitute, my mood swings grow more and more severe. I am homeless, I am alone, I am dependent, I am overwhelmed.

In my journal I write: I have left the marriage.

The Witch at the Wake

The witch is not expected when she walks into the room and starts toward my mother. I move toward her and put my body between them. My sister has come from the other side of the room and we've converged in this place, facing the witch, our mother behind us. There will be no trouble here.

My mother is not aware of what has happened. Kneeling at the coffin, she's saying her last goodbyes to Bob, her husband. She only knows there's been some commotion involving Bob's ex-wife. She lets us put her to bed.

She thought she was going to get there, to get right up beside Ma at the coffin, my sister says. What did she think? We'd just let her?

My brother says it was like watching a basketball play. I saw her come in and I couldn't move, then I saw you two move into defensive position, blocking her from getting at Ma. I couldn't move. I could tell it was a woman's thing. You two just moved to block her, I couldn't believe it, he says. My nieces are looking at the two of us, their eyes wide. We are heroes.

I didn't even think about it, I say. When I saw her walking across the room toward Ma, something inside me just moved. I knew I couldn't let her touch Ma.

Well, she's obviously never had to deal with two strong Indian women before, that's for sure, my sister says.

I am surprised to hear her say this. She is not involved in Native anything, stays away from socials and pow-wows, doesn't go north to meet or visit. Her life is all about the land. She surprises me all the time, my sister.

In the morning my mother gets up early with chest pains. We don't even stop to talk about it, we just get her in the car and drive to the hospital, where they do an EKG, put medicine under her tongue, draw blood, and put her on a drip. The doctors say we've caught it in time, there won't be any damage, but my mother can't go to the funeral. I stay with her at the hospital while my sister goes.

It has been a long day. We are talking about the woman who came unwanted to the wake last night. The woman who was married long ago to Bob, my mother's second husband, dead now from a heart attack.

You know if she'd touched her, Ma would be dead, my sister says.

I know, I know, I say, leaning my elbows on the table, rubbing my temples. My sister gets up and pours us both hot water from the kettle.

She really is a witch, my sister says. Some people are just evil, and she's one. She's evil. That's all there is to it. We swirl our tea bags, watching the water turn from clear, to orange, to brown.

Land of Enchantment II

You have to understand how much people talk about witchcraft in the Southwest. Here in the Northeast, we acknowledge the existence of witches, but we don't talk about it much. In fact, if we do talk about witches, we're talking about the healing kind, strong defiant women. In New Mexico, it seemed that everywhere I went people were talking about witches, forbidden ceremonies that happened down by the river at night. Maybe it was to scare off foreigners like me, maybe not. Witches take pleasure in other people's pain, and causing it is their pleasure. Whirlwinds, dust devils, are somehow connected to witchery—manifestations, or footprints, or even witches themselves riding the hot desert air.

I left the land of enchantment with witchcraft on my trail. I could feel it behind me, sure as the thunderheads breeding tornadoes on the way from Albuquerque to the East Coast. Oklahoma City had just been devastated by a tornado nobody thought could touch such a big city. I slept in a motel that had been spared, wrapped myself in my green summer quilt, patches of leaves and berries, ferns and birds, and slept, protected by the woods and fields of home.

I felt it differently at different times—sometimes a swarm of bees heading toward me, sometimes like a black cloud threatening to reach down its hand, sometimes just a feeling that it couldn't find me, but was looking, looking. I was carrying no ring of power, no secret I could tell, only their dislike of my eyes, which they said could kill with their intensity, calling out their greed and the malice they took out against my students. Their conviction that I did not belong there, my Northeast Indian self doubted, unwanted.

They are right that I do not belong in that place with no water. I pack everything I can fit into the van and get on Route 40. There is a band of tornadoes coming through and I intend to stay well in front of them. I call my sister every night, and all the way through Oklahoma, Missouri, Indiana, Illinois, Ohio, my niece follows my path, keeping track of the tornadoes, until I am safely in Pennsylvania, just hours away from NYC and my sister's home in Connecticut.

I feel strong, free, driving cross-country by myself. I look for diners and eat big breakfasts of eggs, bacon or country ham, homefries, and thick buttered toast. I stock up on yogurt, candy bars, water, and Coke. Find a place to stay and have a burger or sub before bed. I have agreed to drive no more than eight hours a day, so it takes me an extra day to get home, but finally I am crossing the George Washington Bridge, and it is seven miles to my sister's, and finally I am there.

The next day she takes me out on the water. She is conservation director of this wealthy town full of movie stars, Wall Street bankers, and old money. Today she is working on one of the islands offshore. We grab a lift on an old out-of-service garbage scow. The air is full of sea. I absorb it through my skin, breathe it deeply into my lungs.

We are planting flowers with the town's garden club to prepare for the beach's opening day. I tuck in the roots of the geraniums, tamp the soil around them. The island is grassy and treed, and after planting, I walk past the sandy beach, too much like a desert. I walk instead to the rocky beach, the rocks round and wet-shiny, the tide pools full of life.

That is where my sister finds me and hands me a paper cup of lemonade. I am so grateful she doesn't expect me to talk. I feel safe here, nothing chasing me. Water all around, like home, the island where we grew up.

I find a place to stay on a small pond. A colleague is going away for a year, and I stay in her cottage. The pond is being drained this summer, of all summers, but there is still enough water for me to know it is home.

It's when I contact my "friend," who was also my boss, for a recommendation, that I know how badly things have gone wrong. He writes me a letter designed to make sure I'll never get a job. It is clear he wishes me ill. He told me he could feel the presence of his dead mother in places he'd been with her. He'd once told me there was a bond between us, a special connection, that he could find me anyplace we'd ever been together. He'd said that in friendship, but now? It's clear to me, I have to move up to the homeland, go underground. Have nothing to do with any of those western people. Stay hidden.

I don't say his name anymore. I refer to him, if I must, as Grand Poobah. I don't want him to hear me say his name and find me. I pull back from the Native writing community. I am safe here in New Hampshire—he has never been here. I am so glad I never took him up to the White Mountains. Homeland is safe. Still, I have to be careful, I don't know what he can hear, who might give me away.

After a few years, I hear that he has died. But that means nothing. He can still reach out from the spirit world. There is no safety. I stay underground.

you have to be
a little bit
crazy
to live in the crazy
woods you have to
look through the eyes
of the old ones
you have to
sing you have to
call the names
you have to greet
the wind you have to
throw back your head
and howl, you have
to moan, you have to
growl, you have to
sharpen your claws
you have to be
a little bit
crazy

China Doll

When my aunt was in her fifties, she told us a story about a baby-doll she'd had when she was four or five years old. The doll was the old-fashioned kind, with a china head and soft body. She played with the doll for hours, held it and sang to it while her mother made bread, cleaned the kitchen, made beds, did laundry.

Why, she asked us, would my father smash my doll's head on the stove? No matter how drunk he was, how could he do that? I heard her tell the story about the cast-iron stove, the doll's delicate head, and each time she cried like the little girl she'd been, asking, Why? Why?

Now she is in her eighties. Angry, aggressive, mean-tongued, she pontificates and believes herself wise. Her husband was a violent drunk, yet in the recent violence in our family, brother against sister, she was quick to pardon the aggressor, because men and boys are always right, women always in the wrong. Try to see it from his point of view, she tells me.

My Special One

In the year my grandmother retires from work, my brother Ed is born. My mother has had babies every two years since I was four—my sister, Denise, brothers Paul and John. But this baby is different. I am ten, and although I have not yet started to bleed, I feel a rush of maternal feelings. When I rock him, hold him close, sing to him, look into his sweet baby face, I want to envelope him in love. The feeling is sweeter than anything I've ever known. He is my special one.

He is special to my grandmother, too, born in this year of her retirement. She calls him "my boy." He is the lucky baby who has three mothers—my mother, my grandmother, and me.

When he is five, my grandmother gets cancer. At first my mother takes care of her at home. My aunts come over every day; it is a constant coming and going. My sister and I have our own room now and my parents sleep on a new sofa bed in the parlor. We don't share Gramma's bed anymore because she can't stand the pain of being touched.

When she goes to the hospital, it is eight long months of my mother being gone all day, all evening. My brother Ed has only one mother, now, and it's me, a poor substitute, too young to be the real thing, and I am not the one he wants. When Gramma dies, my mother is pregnant with her last baby, one that will bring her back into life, away from sickness and death, and I am happy for her. Her grief is so big it can't allow anyone else's in. She can't see her little one suffering.

When the baby is born, it is all about him. He is a redhead like her. It is her easiest birth, she tells us over and over again. He is a happy child, not colicky, not allergic to milk like Ed was. Ed is too old to be rocked and cuddled. He is going into first grade. He is a big boy.

From the start, he has trouble in school. He gets angry in Little League, has tantrums when he makes mistakes. I come home from classes at the university to find him tearing the arms and legs off his GI Joe, the tires off his toy trucks. He is the unlucky one who gets caught. He lies. He tells impossible stories. He drops his pants to the neighborhood girls and says, How about it? He is just plain bad, my mother says. And in the next breath, He just needs more love.

He perfectly mimics a neighbor from down the road, walking as if he's drunk, collapsing onto the living room rug. He has us in stitches, talking like the trucker he met in the hospital when he's been hit in the eye with an apple my other brother has thrown. He sings descant in the boys' choir and has people crying in the auditorium seats when he is ten, with his portrayal of Oliver, singing "Where Is Love" with such depth of understanding. He could be an actor, I think, on Broadway.

It's not surprising when he starts drinking with his older brothers, smoking pot, snorting cocaine. Not surprising that when they stop, he does not. He lives, with his wife and two daughters, my nieces, in the apartment downstairs in my mother's house, the one she and my father had built for my grandparents. He doesn't pay rent. He doesn't pay utilities. He has free cable. After my father dies, my mother builds a pool in the backyard and expands his apartment, builds him a new kitchen and a huge living room. There's always beer in his fridge, a dime bag on the coffee table.

When my mother is in the hospital, nearing death, it's all happening again. It's me upstairs, staying in my mother's house above his apartment, so I can be at the hospital every day. Soon my mother will be gone, and I will still be here, not the one he wants.

Because I have refused to continue to enable him, to make appointments with therapists he never keeps, have stopped listening to him sobbing his sorrow over the phone about whatever new thing he's done, he tells everyone I hate him, I've always hated him.

He is my special one, so although I've listened to him rant and rage about getting this one and killing that one, I don't expect his violence. Maybe I should, but I don't see it coming.

After Dropping Acid on a School Night

They have driven over on the rainbow road, they tell me, and now my brother is crouched on the back of the sofa like an elf, holding a Kleenex box, throwing one Kleenex into the air after the other, watching them drift to the floor like giant snowflakes, while his friend laughs and throws a pillow over and over at his head. The Kleenex flies up, a pillow bop to the head, the Kleenex floats down. I take out the Parcheesi board, and they are eager to play. This is a rainbow night, they agree, and they decide what colors they will be, which rainbows they are playing on, and how they will tell them apart. I make popcorn, put out sodas, and we play past midnight, and they promise the rainbows are gone and they can get home safe. I watch from the second-floor window of my flat, while they get into the car and drive away through puddles rainbowed with oil.

Yeats

He spends the first two sessions taking a history of my life, my family. He is cold and precise. I feel like a bug under a glass. He is counting every hair, every facet of my eyes, the number of legs and the veining of wings. He can classify me as beetle, wasp, dragonfly.

He classifies me as bipolar. He is wrong, he is wrong, he is wrong.

Not only that, but he sees others in my family who are probably bipolar, too, my grandfather, my brother. And the cousins who've actually been diagnosed bipolar or schizophrenic. But I'm not like them, I say. I don't drink, I don't use drugs, not since college, anyway.

He tells me a story about the poet, Yeats, whose daughter was institutionalized. How he told Jung, the famous psychologist, that he couldn't understand it. She is drowning, Jung told him, in the water you are swimming in.

Do you understand? he asks me. They are self-medicating because they are drowning. You are swimming.

Up north the swirling waters of the Pemi have carved a basin in the granite rock. What does it mean to swim in a whirlpool?

You Bet Your Life

On Tuesday nights when I'm a kid, we watch "You Bet Your Life." There's a man named Groucho, with thick eyebrows and a cigar, who says mean things to people, then asks them questions from a card. There is a secret word every week, and if the people say it, a duck swings down with a note in its bill that tells the amount of money they've won.

Every day while I live at my son's house, there is a secret word. Nobody knows what it is. There are no clues. They walk in the door from work. They are not thinking about the word. It could be laundry or bathroom or homework. It could be kitchen or dishwasher or T-shirt. It could be comic book or video game or Pink Floyd. It could be football or ice cream, supper or television. Maybe it's mail, or rain, or sun, or backyard. Could it be Monday or Saturday, temple or Columbus? Maybe sweater, or football, or Disney World, or airplane.

Whatever it is, I will swoop down like some squawking bird and let them know. There is no money prize. There's no cigar, no big eyebrows, just me, grouchy, full-tilt mean, raging.

Crazy Talk: Lonely

This therapist likes to ask if I ever feel lonely. You spend a lot of time alone, she says. Yes, but when I'm writing I don't feel alone. Well, when do you feel lonely? she asks. At parties, I say. At parties, and in the middle of cities.

So what do you do, then, when you feel lonely, she asks. I go into the woods, I say. I find a brook or a pond and sit on a log or a stump. Yes, she says. She shakes her head impatiently. But you're still alone, she says.

Alone? I'm never alone in the woods.

She doesn't believe me. She sees the woods as a world of objects, what she calls *a romanticized landscape*. She doesn't see it as a peopled world. The maples, oaks, birches, the cattails and reeds, the fish and beavers, the chipmunks, the ants, dragonflies, the deer, bear, even the mosquitoes-all people, all of us together. How could I possibly be lonely here?

She shakes her head. I'm resisting, she tells me, I'm avoiding the subject.

How can she ever help me heal, when she won't listen to what heals me?

Eating Worms I

Nobody likes me, everybody hates me, I think I'll eat some worms . . .

. . . childhood song

Depression means eating worms big time. It doesn't matter if I saw friends yesterday for lunch, or went to a writing group on Sunday, today nobody likes me, I have no friends. And it has always been this way and it will always be this way.

Do not try to reason with me, I know what I know. And what I know is I am totally unlovable. What I know is this aloneness, this deep loneliness, this need for connection has gone on forever. And there is no one, no one in my life. I don't call anybody, because I know they won't want to talk with me.

But you just had lunch with her two days ago, my daughter-in-law says, of course she'll want to talk with you. But there is no convincing me.

Nobody likes me, everybody hates me,
I think I'll eat some worms . . .

My father used to sing this to any of us at the dinner table who was in a cranky mood. Sometimes it would make us laugh, sometimes it would make us cry, sometimes we'd get angry at not being taken seriously.

I can hear him singing this song now, in the background, but it doesn't help.

My Mother's Side

Gramma Rose tells of her mother-in-law, mean and ugly in her ways, crazy in her spirit. It turns out she had rheumatoid arthritis. So maybe she wasn't crazy after all, just crazed by constant pain, angry and overwhelmed.

Maybe it was Rose's husband, Grampa Henri, who died before I was born, whose photo twists my eyes—the two sides of his face do not fit together. The violent healer. The binge drinker, hunting his own children in the lilac garden.

It was his brother, Great-uncle George, who was institutionalized for "excess religiosity." He carried a wooden cross around from church to church, where he went to receive Holy Communion several times a day. The priests told him to stop, that it wasn't right, you could only receive the host once a day. But he kept right on doing it, carrying his cross like a *penitente*, only we don't have those in New England.

I hear him now in my mother's voice at the dinner table when she gets into her religious fervor in my teens, when my father tells her to get off her soap-box. I hear him in my brother's religious fervor—a kind of fundamentalist Catholicism. My brother dreams dreams and has visions. He wonders about the architecture of Heaven.

Ceremony

I am living up north. I am terrified all the time. I don't correspond with anyone in the Native writing community. I spend my days with my Tarot cards, doing spread after spread, trancing out for hours at a time, or sleeping. On good days I get up and make meals.

I still see the young writer I've mentored, who is now getting her doctorate, when she is home from school. We have become good friends. I tell her again that I'm afraid of Grand Poobah. That I never feel safe. I offer to do her cards.

Next time she visits, it is the same story. It's always the same story, and things are getting worse, not better.

What you need, she says, is a ceremony.

And so I am sitting, wearing all the silver I own to deflect evil intentions, to throw them back to where they've come from. We smudge with sweetgrass. We say the words. We build defenses. We ask help from all our relations.

Later, we drive north, into the Whites, where we go down to the river and let it bless us. We walk the healing paths. For the first time in so long, I feel safe. I feel myself again, strong and whole and unafraid.

I visit the mountains often, sometimes just taking off in the middle of the day and coming home late at night. My husband gets used to my comings and goings. The land works its magic. I put the Tarot cards away in their boxes. I accept an invitation to do a poetry reading. I slowly climb up from underground.

Falling into Grace

My grandfather Henri fell off the steeple of St. Joseph's Church. It has always seemed symbolic to me, this falling, a fall from grace and into drink, but it was drink that saved him, his muscles so relaxed that he sustained no injury. Got up and walked home for dinner, the story goes. A miracle.

My Grampa Philip's name was actually Philibert. I'd heard my Gramma Delia call him that during one of their rare moments of tenderness. Filly Bear is what I heard, and I thought it was a pet name, until I saw his birth certificate. By then I'd thought hard about what a Filly Bear was. A young female horse with a bear's spirit? But Grampa was no filly, though he was a Bear. I knew that because he told me we were Bear people, so that was clear enough, and I was sure Gramma hadn't said Silly Bear, though that would have made sense, because Grampa loved to laugh, and when he danced he could mimic everyone else's way of walking—a gift he passed down to my brother, Ed—drunk or vain or stuck up, Grampa would get it dead on.

Grampa Filly Bear liked the Yankees, not the Red Sox, an unheard-of thing here in Red Sox country, and he wasn't even from New York. Why does he like the Yankees? I asked Gramma, and she said, Because he's contrary.

Grampa Filly Bear didn't fall off a church, he walked out of one over some unkindness he would never name, nor would my Grandma Delia tell me the story. Only that he got mad at the unkindness of a priest and vowed never to go to church again. Unkindness. That is the word they used. Unkindness, the unforgivable. Mostly we didn't speak of his absence at Sunday masses and First Communions, how he showed up at wedding receptions, but not the ceremony, not that he had anything against the ceremony itself. It was understood, Grampa didn't go to church.

How we fall from grace. My own fall was into pregnancy, divorce, and then living in sin. My falling out with the Church began when I was fourteen. I'd decided that St. Augustine's Proof of God that the nuns taught us didn't prove anything to me. After following the "who made this and who made that" logic back to who made the universe, and then on to the final question, the point of the exercise, "Who made God?" and the answer that God always had been and always would be, I asked why we had to move out of the universe at all. Why do we have to go from what we know, to faith in something imagined? I thought the words in my favorite prayer, ". . . as it was in the beginning, is now, and ever shall be, world without end, amen" summed it up nicely. There was no need for a god, or maybe the universe itself is God. It is sacred and eternal. I argued that as self-evident.

I was sent to detention to improve my conscience and had to write 250 words about what I'd done wrong, so I wrote out my objections to Augustine's proof of First Cause, and I don't think they read it because they never spoke of it again, and neither did I.

I kept on going to church, first because I was living at home, and then because that's what everyone does, but my heart wasn't in it. So when I found myself pregnant when I was eighteen, by a boy I'd forgotten to break up with, with the threats of giving the baby away in my ears, I got married with the same enthusiasm I'd felt in going to the prom, which I wouldn't have gone to at all, except the senior class had extra money, and it was free. I borrowed a gown, threaded my hair with daisies, and went. I pretty much did the same when I got married, except my mother bought me a gown for fifty dollars on sale, and had the reception at the Chez Ami restaurant where the whole family got to guess whether my breasts had grown because I was pregnant, and what month the baby would be born in.

I'd read in my biology textbook about how hard it is for a sperm to penetrate an egg. That wasn't true in my case. I went from virgin to pregnant in one wild weekend when I would have climbed up the church spire and whooped with high spirits as if what I'd discovered wasn't something everyone else already knew about, as if it hadn't been going on as it had in the beginning, is now, and ever shall be. That night on our honeymoon in a trailer park at Point Judith, I heard bees humming in the wall, and, with the baby resting on my bladder, risked walking out to the unfamiliar outhouse, shining the flashlight around the seat checking for black-widow spiders each time.

I didn't walk out of the Church until later, after the baby was born, when the priest gave a sermon about the evils of interracial marriage and threw in drug-crazed hippies for good measure. Half the congregation was French-Canadian, many French-Indian whether or not they'd admit it. Who did he think he was talking to, using words like *miscegenation*? It was the pure hatefulness of it that marked the time of my exit. I was glad, then, of the story about Grampa Philibert, who'd walked out of the Church fifty years earlier because of something, some other unkindness, he heard out of the mouth of a priest.

My father didn't walk out of a church, though he probably should have when my mother cried about not going to my cousin Joey's wedding to his girl Ginny, who was fifteen and pregnant. The church wouldn't marry them and the priest told my mother it would be a mortal sin to support them living in sin. My father said it was mean-spirited not to support the kids when they were only trying to do the right thing, but he went along with my mother's decision not to go, so she wouldn't worry about him going to hell for the mortal sin of attending a wedding of Catholics in a Protestant church, even if the Catholics in question were practically excommunicated.

After my son was born, after the divorce, I fell farther from any hope of grace when I started living with a Jewish man and then married him. I'd ignored letters from the bishop regarding an annulment, which I thought was stupid. Make up your mind, I said to the air around me, you believe in divorce, or you don't.

And so I got married again. Not in the temple, not in the church—neither of them could make room for us—but in the living room of a

J.P. with a long face and a wife who hovered over the record player and dropped the needle onto the recording of "Here Comes the Bride" at just the right moment. We were both wearing jeans, hiking boots, and snorkel jackets. My son was carrying his favorite stuffed animal, a yellow toy dog. He'd drawn circles around its eyes with black marker, so the dog could have glasses like he did. He stood with his index finger pointed up, as directed, holding the ring so it wouldn't fall off and go sliding across the floor and get lost under some piece of furniture. After we both said I do, the tinny recording of the Wedding March started, and I hid my laughter in my hands because I didn't want to offend the lady who was only trying to be nice.

Churches are easy to fall off or out of—I'm not the only one to think so. I recommend it, in fact, if you want to avoid unkindness and be welcome, especially if you are contrary in any way, falling off a church is the way to go.

My brother sends me letters now and then. I can tell they're from him before I open them, because there's never a return address. He said he prays for me because he knows I'm going to burn in hell. I told him prayer is never wasted.

He told me Jesus talked to him in a dream. I told him Eric Clapton talked to me in a dream, but I don't base my life on it. He asked me one time if I thought God ever changed his mind. I wonder if that means he's had a change of heart about me, and needs to believe God might, too.

When I was in my twenties, doing Buddhist meditation morning and night, and smoking a lot of grass, I realized that if everything is one, then sacred and profane are simply ways of looking at the mystery we find ourselves in. It is a choice, and so I chose, and fell into grace, into the sacred, living, magical world.

A Paycheck Away

This midlife poverty seemed to come out of nowhere—a bad economy, loss of jobs, foreclosure, divorce. This poverty that sent me to government offices, that dictates where I can live and if I get health care, that introduced me to "the system," you know, the "you-can't-beat-the-system" system.

It's different from the outside. You know something's broken. You know there's too much poverty—people are living in their cars, people with jobs. Years ago I saw a documentary of women in California. All of the women interviewed had previously been middle class, the narrator said. One had lived in a house with a swimming pool, one had a job in computers, another had been a teacher. Now they all lived in their cars. How had their lives come to this? The fear that was touched in me was a deep and secret one.

So let's get one thing clear from the start. If losing a job means that one or two or eight months down the road you'll have used up all your savings, you're not middle class. If loss of that job means you'll lose your house, too, you're not middle class. Middle Class is a lie America tells itself. Most of us are just a paycheck away from poverty. We are a working-class and working-poor country, just a paycheck away from losing everything.

Seven Mice

They appear all at once. Mouse turds on the kitchen counter, little piles here and there. I go into tornado mode, whip out the bleach and paper towels, and clean the counters. I move all the bottles of vinegar and oil that don't fit in the cupboard, I wash the cutting boards with bleach. I put anything that can fit into the dishwasher and turn off the energy saver. These things need heat to get them clean.

I try to deal with it myself. I am supposed to be learning to be independent. My friend gives me a mouse have-a-heart trap and some sunflower seeds, with directions to place it along the wall which is the mice's preferred highway, and to flush the mouse when I catch it.

The first night with the trap, I hear a "clink" while I'm reading in the living room. The trap is already warm from the mouse's body. I open the door for a second, see the cute furry face, and I can't flush it. I grab my keys, and walk all the way across the parking lot to the little woods there, and shake the mouse out onto the leaves. I can feel it resisting at first, but it finally falls into the leaves and I walk back to my apartment, feeling relieved that I caught the mouse, and that I so humanely let it go outside.

It's probably a field mouse, I tell myself, that came in because the weather's getting colder. I've only ever encountered field mice. I've never lived in an apartment complex before. In a city. Without cats.

When I get inside, I put more seeds inside the trap, just in case, and go back to my reading. Clink. Within a half hour, there's another mouse in the trap. Okay, so it has a mate. I follow the same route across the parking lot as before, and leave it in the same pile of leaves. I hope they find each other. Who knows what mouse feelings they have? What attachments? I think I've read that rats mate often and indiscriminately. But are mice the same?

I set the trap again when I get inside. When I wake up the trap is still empty. I spend the morning recleaning the counter and stove, under the toaster oven. I empty the dishwasher. When I go to put the silverware away, there are turds in the silverware drawer, so I take out the contaminated silverware and put it in the dishwasher. I clean the drawer with more bleach.

After I take a shower, I'm able to make some lunch without fear of Hanta virus or some other horrible disease. The kitchen is clean. I buy some groceries, put them carefully away. I don't want to leave even a crumb to tempt any mice back in. The next morning I make eggs and bacon in my cast-iron skillet, then carefully clean the skillet with clear water and oil the surface. The skillet is finally seasoned the way I like it, so the eggs just glide off the pan, and the home fries crisp up brown with the sweet onions.

The kitchen is small, with no window, dark, tucked away on the other side of the closet and the bath, which doesn't have a window either. But even without any grace or beauty, I feel good. It's clean, my skillet's on the stove, my wooden drying rack's next to the sink, and my vinegar bottles are gleaming.

I leave to spend a few days with friends. I tell them about the mice and joke about needing to borrow their cat, Marc, who is a good mouser. I've always lived with cats until now, so I've seen mice being chased across the kitchen floor, and I've found their remains outside on the steps, and once had a mother cat bring a live mouse into the house to teach her kittens how to hunt. I shut the door to the kitchen and left them to it. I'm not a very good mouser, I admit. I don't kill them. I just bring them outside.

When I get home, there are turds on the counter again, but that's not all. My black skillet has turds covering the bottom like black rice. I empty it out and scrub it with a brush and dishwashing liquid that I know will ruin the seasoning built up so patiently, but I have to get it really clean. I oil it, then stick it in the oven to bake for a couple of hours. That should kill everything. I let it cool down, wash it with clear water, oil it again, and put it back in the oven so the mice can't get into it.

I reset the trap. And before an hour passes, I catch another mouse. This time I don't take it out to the woods. I flush it, as I was directed. Who knows, maybe those mice I left outside found their way back in.

And so it goes for a few more days. A clean day, a mouse-turd day. One morning the trap is empty, but the crushed almonds I've used for bait have disappeared. Well, I think, the mice are anticoagulated, they won't get little mouse heart attacks. I've been putting off calling the landlord because I don't want an exterminator to come and fumigate. I don't want to live with poisons, and I don't want to set my asthma off. But finally, it gets ridiculous, and I stop at the office when I get my mail.

It turns out the exterminator is coming to my building today anyway, not because of mice, but because of fleas. Great. I think of the bite I had this morning when I woke up. Shit. When the exterminator guy shows up, he sprays poison in the hallway, then comes to my apartment. He says it's unusual for the mice to come on top of the counters. Is he kidding? He puts two killer traps under the sink. He pulls out the drawer of the stove, where mice apparently *like to live*, and puts poison bait behind it. He notices some droppings next to the fridge and puts some bait there, too. He doesn't ask or investigate where the mice are coming from.

The next morning I find two dead mice in the traps he set, drop them into the trash, do my usual cleaning routine, and this time include all the pots and pans from the drawer under the stove. I think it's finally over. Why do I have such confidence? Do I actually believe that some male exterminator has a special power over these mice? I spend the day making quiche, beef stew, raspberry muffins. Everything tastes especially good.

Reading in bed that night, I hear a loud clanking coming from the kitchen. I figure something is out of place in the dishwasher, but when I go into the kitchen, the dishwasher is off. The clanking continues. It's coming from the have-a-heart trap. There's a mouse in there trying to get out, shaking the whole trap. The door of the trap is clanking open and shut. This is how the mouse who ate the almonds must have gotten out the other day.

This time I walk into the bathroom, holding the trap closed. I can feel the mouse still moving inside, feel the heat of its body. But when I hold the trap open over the toilet, the mouse decides to hold on and I can't shake it into the water. Oh, god, it's gonna run up my arm, I think, and slam the trap shut. I take the walk across the parking lot. This time I don't go to the woods, I bring it to the dumpster. Have a ball, I say, as I shake it out into the garbage.

An hour later, the trap clangs again. Did the mice teach each other how to do this? Is there a mouse university somewhere? This one I do flush. And I crawl into bed and dream of rats. There are people who keep them as pets. Are they nuts?

It is an adjustment, learning to live alone. I expected the silence, the changing of light bulbs, carrying in all the groceries myself. I didn't expect to catch seven mice in less than a week.

Christmas with Tarot Cards

My brother says I made my mother cry because I played Tarot cards at Christmas, and it was a sacrilege and a sin, and against God, and from the Devil. I can hardly remember it, but when I ask my sister, she says, It was that Christmas that she bought Tarot cards for her girls. I'd told them about the Major and Minor Arcana, the path from the Fool to the World, and shown them how to do a spread on the dining room table after dinner.

Ma loved it, she said. Ma went to psychics, don't you remember? It was Auntie Doris who had a problem with it, she's the one who made Ma cry. It was Auntie Doris who said, How can you have this blasphemous stuff at your table? And at Christmas, Cecile, really. I don't know what Auntie Doris was thinking, my sister says, she bought us a Ouija board when we were kids.

So what is it about my mother and me that makes our siblings think they can tell us we are wrong? And more than that, that we'll believe it?

Geraniums

My mother is planting geraniums in the new brick planting boxes my uncle has built along the front porch. She carefully takes each plant out of its container, digs into the dark loam, places it carefully in the hollow she's made, and presses her fingers into the soil around it, fixing it in a line of geraniums from one end of the porch to the other.

I hate geraniums. There is something about their garish red balls of blossoms that I don't like. They are the firebell clang that warns of the prickly stems and leaves, the rank smell. I tell her I don't like them, and she tries to convince me. Oh, no, she says, they're beautiful.

The next week, she does the same with the hostas, plants them in a line to hide the retaining wall my father made from cement blocks that separate the yard from the dirt road. They never grow tall enough to hide the wall, they are just a sad, spindly row, their whorl of leaves lost in linearity. I hate them, and I hate that my mother loves them.

In my own garden, decades later, I grow to love hostas in all their variety—the giant ones with dark blue leaves, the white-striped and the crinkled-leaf, planted randomly in the shade or in groupings under trees as if they they'd grown there naturally.

My mother loved the linear, the evenly measured, the symmetrical, the lines of space and thought that made sense of the world, that kept chaos at bay. Like the pews in a church, the desks in a classroom, simple melodies sung in three-part harmony.

One day, in the year before her death, we go out to eat at one of her favorite restaurants in town. She lines up her silverware, moves the plate so it's centered, then looks up as if she's been caught at something. I think I'm a little OCD, she says. Really, I say. Yes, she says, eyeing the curtains across the room. I can hardly keep myself from getting up to fix that pleat, she says. I turn and look, and I can't see the pleat that's causing her distress, but I catch her glancing that way in between bites, unable to relax, unsafe in this uneven world.

I'm not like her. I don't have to straighten the world into lines. I am at home with its irregularities and soft edges. I have my own anxieties. Anything new, for example. I hear Joan Armatrading and I recoil—what is this? Music and poetry, a voice so unafraid to growl and squeak and caress. She scares me. Charles Mingus. I can't make sense of this music, I say. Don't try to make sense of it, just listen, a friend says. That helps. They frighten me. It takes me years of hearing them before I like them, before they are among my favorite musicians.

Any food or product I haven't tried before is a threat. I am the monkey in the snow by the hot spring who won't eat the sweet potato. Don't substitute. I like what I like. If I have put down a book, don't move it. If you have used anything in my kitchen, put it back in the right place. Don't change anything. I have my own kind of lines. Like my mother's, they set the limits of control, between the world that's safe, and the chaos outside.

Citizens for Citizens

Because I'm on SSI, everyone has told me—everyone being my case worker from last year that I no longer have because you're only allowed to have one for a year, my therapist, and my daughter-in-law—I am eligible for fuel assistance.

I'm glad to hear it, because the rent takes up my entire SSI check. I am filing applications for senior low-income housing and getting all the necessary backup documents—birth certificate, license, proof of SSI benefits, social security card, rent receipt, bank account. I put fuel assistance on my "do tomorrow list." It takes me three weeks to get to it because of the housing forms and the mice problem in my kitchen.

When I go to the office, the receptionist looks up at me and says, Do you have an appointment? She is a pretty girl with an ugly face. She hates me just for being here. I didn't know you needed an appointment, I say. She says, Have you ever received fuel assistance before? I say no.

We give out appointments at nine a.m., she says, first come, first served, so get here early. I'm nodding yes. Do you know what you need to bring? she says as an afterthought. No, I say. She swings around and gives me a form. Early, she says again.

I haven't learned yet to have a thick skin when I go into these agencies, and this one is called "Citizens for Citizens," which sounds populist and grass-roots. But it's not. It's one of those places where people need to make you feel like shit because you're poor, because you need the service they're offering, and they don't. I won't cry. I won't let her get to me. But I am tired. I don't want to need their assistance.

Wet Ashes

I am in the closet, hunting for the source of the smell. Something smells like wet ashes. I am sniffing sneakers, on my knees looking in corners, not knowing what I might find.

My nose gets tired and I quit for the moment. What smells like wet ashes except wet ashes? Outside the closet, the floor is strewn with shoes and clothes, towels, blankets, hats—it's very frustrating. Maybe the cat walked through ashes outdoors, and brought the smell inside.

I walk downstairs for a cup of tea, tea always helps. I turn on the stove, grab a teabag from the tin, and the smell hits me again, wet ashes. I open and sniff the tin. Nope. Just tea. But the smell of wet ashes is strong in the kitchen, stronger than it is upstairs, and now I am under the sink, moving Windex and rubber gloves, dishwashing detergent, spray bottles and bleach, dried-up sponges—nothing wet, no smoky carbon smell.

I never find the source, although it comes back frequently. I go down to the cellar, search around our old furnace, but it is warm and dry—the old soapstone sink has a spiderweb, but the faucet isn't leaking. Then I notice there's laundry on the floor. Something in the pile might be the problem. I start sorting and sniffing. And then the smell is gone. In fact, I can't smell anything, my nose has shut down.

Sometimes I wake up in the middle of the night and smell it. I can't believe it is so strong that it wakes me up. This damn house is haunted with the smell of wet ashes. My husband says he can't smell it, but he can't smell anything. What I need is my son here—he's got a nose like mine.

I talk to him on the phone. What can make a smell like wet ashes, I ask him.

Uhhhh, wet ashes, he says.

Very funny, I say.

I don't know, Ma, it's midnight. Go to sleep.

I was sleeping. The smell woke me up.

It's probably nothing. It'll be gone in the morning.

What if there's a fire someplace?

There's no fire, Ma, that wouldn't smell wet. Maybe you were dreaming. Go back to sleep.

I go back to bed. My husband is snoring. I imagine him a fireman—but they shower at the station. Even firefighters don't bring home the smell of wet ashes.

I hate not knowing. It's like walking into the kitchen in the morning and smelling something rotten. The first thing you have to do is hunt down the bad onion, the lone potato left in the bin. Wet ashes follow me around for years. No matter how hard I hunt, I never find the source. I wear people out, talking about it.

I can't smell it, Ma. It's in your imagination.

I guess I know when I'm smelling wet ashes, I tell him.

In my midfifties, I tell my therapist about it in passing.

Do you know there are olfactory hallucinations? she asks me. Smells that aren't really there. It's very common in people with bipolar illness. Some people get them with migraines.

Maybe the shrink is wrong. Maybe wet ashes is the smell of the passion going out of my marriage, the cold remains of love and anger.

It might be a hallucination. But here's the thing. When I leave the marriage, when I get a divorce, the smell of wet ashes goes away.

The Eighth Mouse

There's a clanging in the kitchen again. It seems to be coming from the stove area. When I approach, the clanging stops. I figure it's a mouse behind the stove, hopefully eating the poisoned bait. When I turn my back to leave the kitchen, the clanging starts again.

It's definitely the stove. While I'm listening, I notice the plastic bag I have hanging from the oven door's handle. It has a tuna fish can in it and I figure I will tie it up and take it out to the dumpster so it doesn't smell up the kitchen. As I tie up the bag, the tuna can clanks against the stove. I stop. I swing the bag gently against the stove. Clank. That's the sound. I take the bag out to the dumpster, and the clanging stops and doesn't come back.

I never understood the expression, "Don't let the cat out of the bag." Cats like to be in paper bags, why bother them? And what happens if you let them out? I think the expression should be, "Don't let the mouse out of the bag." Tie it closed and take it to the dumpster.

This is not the end of the mice. There might never be an end to the mice. I don't know because after mouse thirteen, I get a call from Easton Housing Authority. We have an apartment for you, she says. You're an emergency. No kidding, I think. I hang up and sob my relief.

And just like that, I'm moved, and the apartment is clean. Mice wouldn't stand a chance here. I've brought my cast-iron skillet with me. It's in the closet. Every once in a while, I take it out and put it on the stove. But I can't bring myself to cook in it. Every time I do, I see it full of turds. I know it's clean, but I can't help it, and finally, I throw it out.

Good morning:

I am writing to tell you that I am moving out of my apartment at the end of the month. I am living on SSI, which is just about the same as the rent, and I cannot afford to continue payments. I have just been offered and accepted a subsidized apartment in a senior housing complex.

Another reason I have to move is that I have had an ongoing problem with mice, which was not resolved by the exterminator. I have continually had to clean my kitchen with bleach. The mice and their droppings, as well as pesticide used in the hallway to kill fleas, have aggravated my asthma, not to mention my peace of mind.

The lighting in the hallway and exits has often been out, which is very unsafe for me, especially with the stairs as I have a knee problem.

Thank you for your attention to this matter.

Sincerely,

Memere Stories: Paint

Every day, when I paint, I set out water and brushes for Adam and Joey. I show them how it works, to wet the page and make beautiful washes. To paint on dry pages to make sharp or scratchy lines. I've bought them their own paints, non-toxic, and good big brushes. We use sticks to make scraggly lines, and toothbrushes to spatter. We sprinkle salt and wait for it to dry, then brush it off to see what's happened. We use sponges and crumpled paper, meshes and doilies, to make patterns. Joey loses interest, but Adam is lost in color and water. He paints three, four paintings one after the other. Then he is done.

I live with them, sharing Adam's bed, for over a year. Then for almost another year, I live a few towns away, and see them only once in a while. When I move into a new apartment nearby, he comes to visit. He spots my paints and says, Let's make art! and spends the next hour painting at the small table in the living room. When he leaves, the wall is spattered with paint that I don't wash off.

Not Connect: Abilify Mania

I am becoming more and more manic. Yesterday I went shopping with my five-year-old grandson and bought two bags of clothes I didn't need, with money I should use for food. That looks nice, Memere, he said, while I tried on clothes, I like that one.

I can't seem to stop moving around. This may be what the doctor meant when he talked about the med making me feel like I want to walk around all the time. I think he meant I couldn't stay still.

I'm not thinking straight. I can't seem to connect A to B. I can't even connect A to A. I need to walk this off, I need to move, my body is not mine, it is a puppet to this need to move.

I wish somebody was here. I take an extra lorazepam in hope it will calm me down, but it doesn't. I try to sleep—but I can't sleep, not with this something grinding away inside me.

I still can't stop moving around. That must be what the doctor meant when he said I might want to walk around all the time. I think he meant I couldn't stay still. Is this what he meant?

I hate when a med makes it worse—it fulfills all my dread of new meds—dread of meds, dread of meds—what the fuck's this rhyming shit about?

I'm going to watch TV downstairs, if I can just stay calm. I'm going to pack up and go home tomorrow. When I get like this, Chris can usually talk me down. But it's late and I don't want to bother him.

I call my ex-husband and tell him I can't stop moving around. I tell him I don't know who else to call. I think it's the new med. He talks me down. He says he'll always consider me family, forever, and that I can call him anytime. I know my son and my sister would be pissed that I called him. They'd remind me about his lies, his emotional abuse, that he encouraged me to be sick, but oh, well. My relationship with him is my own business. Besides, who else can I call who knows me like this?

Why can't I stop moving around? That must be what the doctor meant when he said I might want to walk around all the time. I think he meant I couldn't stay still. Is this what he meant?

After the phone call, I fall into a deep sleep. I wake up scared—how could I have fallen asleep when I can't stop moving? What if that happens again? What if I go into a coma? I am pacing the floor back and forth with each question, what if, what if, what if I die here?

At no time do I consider calling 911. I am supposed to call 911 if I get manic, but I never even think, This is mania, I'm manic, never mind, when am I manic enough? I just can't stop moving. My ex didn't mention calling 911 either. I could die right in front of him and he'd still be considering whether he should call the ambulance.

In the morning, I get in the car with a bag of new clothes, point it toward home, and drive. It's all I can do, just point the car, and drive.

Piano

On the day my husband loses his job, I start to shop for a piano. My own piano, a Baldwin Acrosonic, like the one I grew up playing, was one my mother found for me when I wasn't even looking. Listen, she said to me on the phone. There's an Acrosonic for sale—call right away. And so I did, and bought the piano, with the same soft touch and mellow tone of my mother's piano, from an elderly couple whose children had grown up. Now there's nobody here who plays, they said. They wanted the piano to go to a good home, and had me play it for them. They were happy, I was happy, and the piano came home with me.

Since then, she had survived a trip to Albuquerque and back. During the move, her leg was broken, which had me screaming at the movers, who had held back the piano for last. The leg got a little messed up there, one of them pointed out. A sound, half gasp, half moan, came out of my mouth. They look at me, unmoved, waiting for instructions. Anyone who doesn't respect a musical instrument has no soul, I spit at them, running my hand along the curves of her broken body.

The leg was fixed, but the dried-out woods, the sound, could not be healed. Some keys get stuck, some buzz. Some notes are silent, and some don't stop and create a discordance that blurs the melody and chords. The pedal is broken. But I check the soundboard, and it still looks solid, no cracks, so I decide to find someone who can take on the work of bringing her back to health. She would be sound, and I would no longer wince or cry out when I tried to play.

I call a piano doctor, who comes recommended. He is a little old man. He tells me he can't fix the keyboard without taking it to his shop. I am holding my head in my hands, I can't look, as he removes the entire keyboard to his truck. When he returns, he can't get the keyboard back into the piano properly. It is worse than before. She will never be sound again.

I have been grieving this loss. Now it is clear to me. I will find a new piano. With my husband out of work, I need a piano more than ever.

My husband has lost jobs before. And ultimately gone through all our savings before finding another, with nothing to show for it. At least this time, I will have a piano. He's getting unemployment, and I have a little money my mother left me. It seems perfectly logical to look for a piano now—things always turn around.

I begin with the local piano stores, where they know me. I buy sheet music there, Chopin, *Phantom of the Opera*, the latest *Real Book*. I have played most of their pianos. None of them are really right. Most of them are Japanese-made, they are all pretty much alike, all pretty good, but no individual quirks, nothing spectacular. And certainly never the tone that resonates with my soul, that makes me take in a breath, eyes closed, that invites me to play.

There are always some used pianos in the basement, mostly old uprights. What's good about them is that they have a full harp—so it's possible one of these could be the one. But no. They are all disappointments.

In order to have my old piano completely redone, I would have to spend $10,000. I have figured that the least I will have to spend to replace it is $7,000, which seems reasonable for a used piano. But there are no used pianos that have what I want. None of them has that aliveness, that sense of a soul in the instrument. None of them is as good as my old piano.

Pretty soon I start scouting out other stores, driving through southern New Hampshire, then looking online for stores in Boston and New Jersey. I buy books about choosing used pianos, the differences in sound, tone, the light or heavy touch, the brightness or lack of it. I find out about woods—Sitka spruce from the Pacific Northwest for the soundboard because of its acoustic qualities, and sugar pine from Northern California for its strength and flexibility. Hard rock maple from the Adirondacks for the rim, and yellow birch from the Appalachian Mountains for the caps of the keys. A geography of North American forests. I study the way the woods are aged and for how long. How the wood is coaxed into curves. The way they are crafted, or, in the case of the Japanese pianos, assembly-lined.

I play a lot of pianos. At each store I walk by the spinets. Their sound is too small and I have a huge family room now that can easily accommodate a bigger piano. I try the uprights, but most are disappointing. There are some that are great for that tinkly barroom sound, but what if I want to play Mozart?

So I move on to the baby grands. I have always wanted a baby grand. I sit down at the first one, full of anticipation. But it is not splendid. It is not full of resonant sound. I try several more. Still, I find none that really please me. I leave disappointed. Later I read that baby grands have the same size harp as an upright, not as big as a grand. So it seems, if I'm going to buy a grand of any kind, it should be a real grand.

I persevere. I go to more shops. I don't go to the big Steinway store in Boston. I know that if I play one of $100,000 pianos I will never be happy with anything else. And I'm not even a great piano player. I am passingly mediocre. Not really a piano player at all. But it doesn't matter, it is between me and my piano and the music we make together, the time we spend in search of beauty.

As I move on to other pianos, the price goes up. None of them seems undoable. When I start looking at $18,000 pianos, I check in with myself. That's when I decide buying a piano is more prudent than buying a car. It is an investment. Its worth will grow like art or a Persian rug, neither of which I have—they cost a lot of money. We've bought cars before and paid them off in five years, and don't they, even the best of them, eventually turn into junk?

But I still haven't found the one that sings to me, the one I can fall in love with, who will answer my caresses with moans, sighs, murmurs, or crashing thunders, who will forgive me for wrong notes, who will call to me during wakeful nights, who will soothe my dog during thunderstorms, lead me down melodic paths, and teach me how discordance can become harmony.

In a small town, twenty miles from home, I find her. I have been playing old standards on the other pianos in the store. They are all compliant, but the notes do not expand and come together again like breath. There is no brightness, or there is too much. The touch is too hard or too light. They are ordinary. I am ordinary.

There is a piano on a dais—I have been throwing my eyes at her. She is sure of her beauty, the wood deep with luster, the curves breathtaking. She is not a baby, she is full grown. I have circled her, playing other pianos, but always gazing her way as I leave each of them behind.

This lady knows her worth. I am half in love before I sit on the bench, while I rest my hands gently on her keys, then lift them and pause before I begin to play. Please, I think to myself, and play the first chord.

Here is the voice I've been waiting for. I lift my hands from the keyboard for a moment—they are filled with electricity. She has been waiting for me as I've desired her. We are lost in the music; this is the way it's supposed to be. Finally I surface and see the salesman smiling at me.

She's a beauty, he says. I resent him talking about her like that. That's an understatement, I say to myself. She is a soul mate.

I can barely leave the store, can barely talk to the salesman about financing. Thirty-four thousand dollars. It's not so much. I have a cavernous living room that's been waiting for something to anchor it, to fill its vast emptiness. She will bring her weight, her girth, her voice to fill this space.

Thirty-four thousand dollars? my husband says.

Yes.

He tips his head to the side, like a dog wondering if he's heard right. It's a lot of money, he says.

Well, actually, not so much, think how much a car costs. I go into my argument, each point sounding logical, the investment, the ease of payment over several years, the lifetime of pleasure, an heirloom to pass down.

Plus, I say, you have to continually buy gas for a car, pay taxes on it every year, maintenance, car insurance—it all adds up to a lot more than a tuning twice a year. I am sure of myself, it's a foolproof argument, and I argue eloquently. Pretty soon he is agreeing with me, and I go to bed happy, full of anticipation.

When I wake up, it is with the realization that we have no money. My husband has no job. What was I thinking?

I am overcome with grief. I'll have to tell the salesman, but I'll have to tell him as if it just happened last night. I'll call him. I cannot see her again, I would totally break down. I go to bed. I don't know how long it is before I get up.

Memere Stories: Talking

Every afternoon, I pick up Adam from preschool. I no longer live in the big house with him and his parents, since his Zayde and I have split up. He comes to my new apartment with its small red living room that fits just a couple of chairs and my piano. Every day we go down to the big back yard, walk the path through the perennial garden, looking for bunnies, picking just one flower each day. We walk down to the compost pile, and throw in yesterday's leavings, scoop a shovelful of soil on top, then walk back to the porch where he sits in the white rocking chair. I bring out a snack of peanut butter and jelly, or cookies and milk. Later, he sits at the piano while I'm busy in the kitchen or folding the quilt from his nap. He plays with abandon and focus. Slow, pensive movements that become louder and more insistent, then happy tinkling sounds down the keyboard. He calls out to me. Memere, he says. Can you hear me? Yes, I say. It's lovely. When I play the piano, Memere, he says, it's like I'm talking to you.

if I
hear voices
if I
see visions
if I don't
play well
with others
if I
need silence
and trees and
water
the sounds
of birds, the snap
of beaver tails
if stories and songs
are what come from
my lips when I am not
sleeping like a bear or
roaring like a cougar
will they call me
crazy?

Talk Doc: Karen

After the crazy unkempt shrink who's cast me as a sideshow performer or standup comic, after the twenty-five-year-old caseworker who asks me questions from a form each time she visits: When is the last time I ate? Am I getting dressed every day? Have I gotten out of the house? On a scale of one to ten, what is my mood today? On a scale of one to ten, what has my mood been for the week? Am I having suicidal thoughts? After the ADD guy and the homophobic rich bitch, I tell the woman at the Northeast Mental Health center that I need to see someone older, someone who has worked with people who have bipolar, who isn't homophobic, a woman with experience. She listens, she is sympathetic.

Karen is my new Talk Doc. She is in her forties and has two children. She is French, married to an Italian—there's a chance she'll get me culturally. She's wicked smart. She doesn't cast me in the role of entertainer, but she does have a sense of humor and the absurd.

I am feistier now. I tell her what I need from a shrink. She nods, she's talked with the woman at Northeast Mental Health—she's got notes written in my chart.

I talk a lot, testing the waters; will I be able to swim here, float, is there a safe harbor? She listens, she doesn't flinch under my questions. Yes, she's worked with people with bipolar, but she doesn't like labels, they're too simplistic, everyone is different. I decide to trust her. With her, I start the journey that will bring me back to myself.

Listenings

At Morrow Bay, I wake up to the sounds of birds conversing. It is like hearing someone speaking in the next room. I can almost make out what they're saying, but not quite. I wish I knew the language of birds.

Sometimes my mother speaks to me. It's usually when I'm doing some quiet thing, like making a bed, baking a pie, staring into space at my computer. It is never profound, she never says much, just my name. *Cheryl*, I'll suddenly hear, as if she's calling me, not from far away, but just to get my attention. I stop whatever I'm doing, I listen for more. But it is still. I nod my head and smile. I go back to smoothing the sheets, crimping the pie crust, my fingers start typing.

I wake at night to hear a baby crying. I get up, feel my feet on the rug, move toward the bedroom door. The crying stops. I remember, the baby's not here. I go back to bed. He will be coming over tomorrow for the whole afternoon. I'll be ready.

There's a Sunday cookout at my mother's house. She calls me to come inside with her, but instead of the kitchen, she heads toward her bedroom, shuts the door, and begins to cry. I'm so worried about you, she says. What's happening in your life? Is something wrong?

There is so much wrong, but I don't tell her. She says she had a dream about me. I was out in the ocean, swimming toward shore. My grandmother was standing on the beach, shouting to me, Just a little farther,

Cheryl, you can make it, just a little farther. My mother says she wanted to help, but she couldn't move, she was just an observer.

It's okay, Ma, I say. I've been going through a bad time. Memere always visits me in my dreams when I'm in trouble, but I haven't been sleeping, so I guess she visited you. It's okay. My mother is still crying. Is there anything I can do? she whispers. You have, you've given me the message. I'm okay, really, Ma.

My grandmother has told her what I need to hear. If I keep on swimming, there will be a shore.

Giving Myself to Beauty

They are talking on the radio about Cape Cod National Seashore, and I'm remembering the beaches in September, empty of crowds, the white sand, the gulls, the terns and sandpipers. The cedar maple swamp trail where blueberry bushes grow over your head, the cranberry bog where you have to dodge the poison ivy, the sea turtles by the side of the road, the dunes and the marsh grasses, and the light that Barry Lopez compared to Arctic light, beyond bright.

The National Park Service is going to replace the roads that wind through the dunes and grass with straight four-lane roads. The little roads are part of the charm, part of what makes the Cape special in the first place, one voice argues.

I love those little roads on the Cape that wind naturally with the land, the turns and rises, pitch pines and grasses, and dunes all around until suddenly you're at the sea. On the radio, another voice says, But four-lane roads are standard for National Parks. After a while, I can't listen anymore.

The ugly-makers, the destroyers. It is not enough that they cut the forest down to feed the glass factory and created this desert of dunes. Most people think this is natural, because the land heals, adapts, transforms itself and becomes another kind of beauty. Still, these dunes are blowing away. Every year, people plant young pines that hold the sand with their roots, but it is slow going. And now, with earth's temperature rising, this place will soon be reclaimed by the sea.

I hear the voices waging paper wars against the Land. I decide there is nothing more important than giving myself to Beauty.

The Green Quilt

The palette is mostly grey-greens and browns, very subdued, with some turquoise, gold, orange, and mauve. The woods on an overcast day, instead of in bright sun. Colors that disappear.

I am working in layers, cutting things off, appliquéing over what I don't like. I add a diagonal strip of rocks for tension, a small piece of light turquoise with wisps of cloud, and there's water in a block. Later I will add small pieces over the whole quilt, like confetti, to hold it together. I'm trying to keep in mind that this initial piecing doesn't have to be the total result, but rather is a base to be overlaid.

The blocks have become mini-landscapes, the layering of fabrics like the layers of the woods. I want people to feel as if they can walk into each block. These totally free-pieced blocks have houses, rivers, chimneys— some of it intentional, but some came serendipitously, appearing as if by magic.

I add darker stone walls, sew diagonal strips across several blocks. The stone walls are broken and meandering, and the darkness of the stone, in contrast to the lighter stonework in some of the other blocks, makes them seem damp. I like the way the eye follows the stone wall, or the water, and stops at individual trees or houses or other spots, then moves on.

The clumps of birches are mostly appliqué, but one is pieced into the block. I use a black and silver metallic thread and sew a blanket stitch with fairly wide stitches to mimic the bark markings. I add another clump for balance and because the log cabin block is too dark and overbearing. The golden river birches lighten it up.

I have to rip out the satin stitch on the tiny triangular appliqué. The center block I was having trouble with is now in the upper right corner—it was too subdued for the center but works well as a corner block. The center block pulls you in, like an opening in the trees.

I am starting to see how to put the whole thing together, using some straight edges, but keeping the free quality of the irregular blocks. I attach some pieces of stone wall with safety pins. The illusion of ownership.

Memere Stories: Howling

We've just finished dinner and we're sitting around the table, my grand-sons and I. We are talking about the wolves disguised as coyotes we've heard howling over the hill. Joe, who is five, howls to demonstrate what they sound like. Adam, just two, follows his lead. And then I join in and there are three of us howling together, filling the evening kitchen with song. My daughter-in-law comes in from another room, looking worried. She stops when she sees all of us together, howling, our heads thrown back, our voices overlapping, rising and falling, wolves around the dinner table. The boys see her and grin between their howls, their eyes lit with moonlight.

Eating Worms II

Nobody likes me, everybody hates me, I think I'll eat some worms . . .

. . . childhood song

Depression means eating worms big time. It doesn't matter if I saw friends yesterday for lunch, or went to a writing group on Sunday, today nobody likes me, I have no friends. And it has always been this way and it will always be this way.

Do not try to reason with me, I know what I know. And what I know is I am totally unlovable. What I know is this aloneness, this deep loneliness, this need for connection has gone on forever. And there is no one, no one in my life. I don't call anybody, because I know they won't want to talk with me.

My daughter-in-law knows better now than to argue with me. Instead she says, Do you remember when you were depressed last time, you used those exact same words?

She says, I think this is your depression talking.

I grumble at her, but I think, she may be right. Didn't we agree that when I use those words, *nobody likes me,* that she should tell me?

She has listened to what I said. She is talking, but what I hear is her singing like my father at the table, *I think I'll eat some worms.*

Greeley Park, Nashua—The Tree

With these curling branches leaning toward the ground, it makes a room beneath its canopy. It is a wigwam tree, a living house. It is adult-size, this room under the tree. I thought I'd lost this pleasure of childhood forever. I stand on the picnic table to reach a branch. Our memories of living in the trees, coming from the trees, must be deep in our DNA. I climb up on the table without a thought, as if I am a child. People are watching. What do they think of this fifty-one-year-old woman up on a picnic table leaning on a branch thicker than her thigh? They'd know better if they came up here themselves.

Maura's Bag

Tonight I'm jittery and agitated. I was on the computer at the library for two hours this afternoon, then I came home, played video games, watched TV, took my meds. Reading usually calms me down, but I am skipping from Austen to Erdrich to *The Emperor of All Maladies* and I'm still jittery. I decide to play a video game and realize it's all this artificial light, so I get out the bag I'm making for Maura and do some hand-sewing on the straps.

I'd forgotten the peace of handwork, of sitting quietly with myself, making something beautiful. I don't want music or anything to distract me— just the multicolored stripes of the twill fabric, the folding of edges, the pinning, the needle catching each fold with invisible stitches.

I've made so many excuses for not taking out the machine. It's not because I don't want to sew. And it's not because I'm depressed, because I'm not. It's because I don't want to work with a machine in that awful position that will leave me with a backache for days. The machine's speed turns the peace of creating into work. And machine-sewn straps are clumsy. Much better to hand-sew. Better for the bag. Elegantly finished. I let my spirit flow through my hands.

Talk Doc: The Real Work

I'm not trembling. I still have mood swings day to day, but they are not as strong, I don't feel swept away. I'm not having panic attacks or worrying about having panic attacks, which is almost as bad as the attacks themselves. When I first started therapy, I cried almost the entire visit. It was as if I'd saved it up, as if I needed a witness. Every Wednesday at ten o'clock, I'd sit in the easy chair in the corner by the window, Kleenex box on the table next to me. Now, Wednesday mornings, we talk about my week. The highs and lows, the challenges, the victories, the failures.

How are you feeling? she asks today. Okay, I say. Better.

How are your mood swings?

Less. Still there, but less.

The drugs, she tells me, have brought me this far.

Now, she says, the real work begins.

Relearning the Habits of Childhood

Wake up. Get out of bed. Pick your clothes up off the floor. Tie your shoes. Brush your teeth. Clean the toothpaste off the sink. Take a shower. Wash your hair. Hang the towel on the rack.

Break an egg. Toast the bread. Pour the tea. Sit at the table. Put the milk back in the fridge. Turn the stove off under the kettle. Rinse out your glass. Wash the egg yolk off the plate. Wash the cereal off the bowl.

Throw away the empty ice cream carton. Throw away the empty cereal boxes. Throw away the empty cookie trays. Throw away the used tea bags. Sweep up the potato chip crumbs. Clean up spills. Do the dishes. Take out the trash.

Don't go outside in your nightie. Put on a shirt. Put on pants. Find some socks. Find some shoes. Go outside. Take a walk. Put on PJs. Turn off the TV. Go to bed. Turn off the light.

Old habits lose their hold. What was automatic, isn't. In the book it says, choose one small thing in your life to change. If you do it every day for three months, it will become a new habit. You won't have to think about it, you'll just do it automatically.

I start a list, there are so many small things. Meanwhile, I have to think, I have to remember what to do.

Wake up. Get out of bed.

Crying for Real

Sometimes there's a lot of crying, sometimes there's none. It is hard for me to be touched by anything. It is all me, me, me. There is at the same time too much, a sense of being overwhelmed, and nothing, an emotional numbness.

This crying is a one-way circuit. I picture the string from inside to outside, the cord on which the crying travels. But it doesn't go anywhere, doesn't connect. There is no healing, only desperation. It is one-dimensional, trapped in the self-centeredness of the illness, that says pain pain pain. Like an infant wailing in the center of its wants, I am unaware of anything else.

So it's a surprise when it happens.

I am watching a movie, or the news, or reading a book, and my eyes are full of tears. I'm crying for someone besides myself. I'm crying because of someone else's pain. How long has it been since I've been able to do that?

For a while, I cry all the time, as if I am pregnant, that dipping down into the waters that hold us all. All the sadness and pain, and the terrible beauty of the world, flow from my eyes. After so many years, I'm crying for real.

Horse Dream II

I am following my cat Bessie through the woods, her ears like the ears of a lynx, her coat the grey on grey of the Maine coon cat. She is the sensitive cat, the scaredy-cat of my three, but she is intrepid in these woods. She ducks under fallen branches and through bright green moss, her legs half hidden. She is moving through these woods towards something I can't see. Branches snap at my face, vines wrap themselves around my calves, as I follow her. She is moving into a glade, there is sunshine, there is a cabin, and then she is gone. One of my brothers sits on the steps and I follow him inside. They are all there, my brothers. It is their domain. The wood floors are worn, the furniture is old. They have beards and are wearing jeans and plaid shirts. I sit in a wooden rocker, and my brother straddles my lap. I jump up and escape down the stairs. There is a barn in the cellar. They are dappled grey horses, and they are starving. Some are deformed—broken limbs have grown crookedly back, their backs are swayed, teeth broken, eyes bloodshot. There is sunshine coming in through the windows. I release them from their stalls, throw the barn doors open. We walk into the forest. Broken and wounded, together we will be whole.

Math Games

I am on the computer, playing a game where you use numbers as clues, and make pictures on graphs. It is soothing. No words, just this graph, this filling in of squares.

It is very German, I think, this fascination with numbers. This following of orders, these straight rows and columns. It is very German. Too German. I start to feel anxious. This is what they make people do, I think. This is how the Nazis got people to do things. There could be SS agents right now, watching me through secret cameras. Looking over my shoulder. The SS will be here any minute.

This is a symptom, I tell myself. It is 2013. There is no SS coming.

Still, I am nervous. I stop playing. I go into the kitchen and make myself some tea. I peel a banana, make toast covered with butter. Ahhhh. That's better. I look out the window where the orange lights are stealing the night. I wish I could go out and look at the stars, but it is a long walk into the dark of the sheep pasture.

Finally, I decide to go back to the computer. I play Plants vs. Zombies, but it's a shooter game, time is crucial, the adrenaline is flowing. So I go back to the math game.

I like the monotony of it. The setting up of dots in little compartments until they make a picture. It's actually very English, this game . . .

Meditation—Fern

I count my breaths and feel the connection from womb to earth. I follow each breath, its flowing and receding like the waves on a beach. Thoughts flow through me like clear water and disappear. I have no desire to pursue them. I don't have to follow any road.

I am breathing from my hara, from my belly, from my womb. I sit, breathing with gratitude, with the knowledge that my truest self is unfolding like fiddleheads in the marsh. I don't have to do anything to speed them along—they will unfold until they become themselves.

Ambien: The Butterfly, Lock, and Key

Today when I go over to the kids' house, I try to get my key into the keyhole and it won't fit. I try over and over, turn the key upside down, bend down to look at the lock, which does look as if it might have been tampered with, but it was obviously not recent. Maybe I have the wrong key. I look at my key ring and it is the only key I have other than my house key, my car key, and my mail key. But I did leave my keys with my brother last week—could the key possibly have been lost? But I didn't take any keys off the ring, I left the whole bunch with him.

I try again, this time the other lock, the one on top. My key fits into that, I can move it back and forth—why would it fit in this lock? I try the lower lock again. Finally, I call Marci and tell her I can't get into the house. My key won't work in your door, I tell her. Is it the right key? she asks me. I think so, I tell her. It's the only key not for my house or car.

Then I tell her, it does fit into the top lock, though. She pauses, then says, we only use the top lock. Okay, thanks. I hang up the phone. I try the key in the top lock, and now I remember how to turn the key, first to the left, then all the way to six o'clock to the right, then push the door open.

I am freaked out. I lived in this house for a year, have been visiting and using this lock regularly for the past two years since I've had my own apartment. Over and over again, I've opened the door with the same key in the same lock. Today I forgot how.

I'm afraid to even write what I'm afraid of. Nobody in my family has had dementia. Is this somehow part of bipolar? Did I have a TIA in my sleep? Are my meds causing this? Is this from the new drug? I remember now how a couple of weeks ago, after starting this new drug, I looked at the door of my car, and it was if I'd never seen it before. Which button was the lock, which for the windows? Where was the handle to get me in and out?

I've stopped taking it, I tell my Med Doc. Good, he says. It's a side effect, he says. It could become permanent if you didn't stop the med. He didn't think it was important to tell me this side effect ahead of time. Just try it for two or three days, he'd said. Then call me. On TV, a butterfly promises sleep.

This is not a drug for cancer, or to stop a heart attack, or for hepatitis, or hundreds of other life-threatening conditions. It would've been nice if I'd known the risk, that's all I'm saying. I could've weighed that with the benefits—on the one hand, a full eight hours, on the other hand, short-term memory loss. That doesn't sound bad, short-term memory loss. Except it doesn't mean the memory loss is short-term. It means you lose your short-term memory. Forever. You lose your mind. This lie of a butterfly, gently lulling me to sleep. It would've been nice to know.

I stop the med, but I don't stop worrying. Maybe I have early onset Alzheimer's. Just because I have bipolar doesn't mean I'm safe from other illnesses. Didn't someone say people with bipolar are statistically more likely to get Alzheimer's?

I tell myself, It's from the med. I've stopped the med. It's from the med. I've stopped the med.

SAD

In Alaska, new studies show, traditional people don't get Seasonal Affective Disorder. They sleep more in the deep of winter, when the world is dark and full of snow, and with the long days of summer, they may stay up all night long. When they go to work in the cities and work a nine-to-five day, they get SAD just like everyone else.

This makes perfect sense to me. I stop worrying about sleep. I sleep like a bear in January and work my way into early morning once spring comes. When my doctor asks me how I'm sleeping, I say, Fine.

Nearly Normal

So today in therapy, at the very end of the session, I'm talking about this memoir I'm writing, that I want to call part of it, "Nearly Normal." That being Bipolar II is nearly normal, that it's not like Bipolar I, where you have lots of time in between dramatic episodes, rather than this constant low-grade niggling.

Karen, my therapist, says, Is that what you think, that you have Bipolar II? I'm surprised, and say, Yes, I guess so, except that doctor I didn't like at South Shore said I was Bipolar I.

Karen says that she also thinks I'm Bipolar I, though she says, You know how I feel about diagnoses. Which is that no one is really in any particular box—it's just shorthand for what is very personal. But still.

She said, You're medicated—you respond to medicine like a Bipolar I.

And I realize that, yes, I am medicated. That, yes, I still rapid-cycle, especially when I'm over-tired or stressed. And that, in fact, we've just discussed irrational feelings and thoughts while I played a math game on the computer. This is very German, I thought, frightened by the thought of German SS troops. This is very English . . .

I've also been having a harder time than usual getting myself out of books and movies. There's always this afterglow—when we're still tied up in the world of the story. But that's not the same as wondering what

Hildegarde is doing now, days after reading a novel about Hildegarde von Bingen.

I guess I've been minimizing what are pretty big swings—I'm more like Bipolar II when I'm medicated. That is, I swing from manic to depressed, instead of Manic to Depressed.

Memere Stories: Baseball

Joey loves to move, loves to run, loves balls from before he can hold one. He rolls the big blue ball around on the floor, kicks it, while he's still holding on to the furniture. His first word is not Mama, is not Daddy, it is Ball.

He loves to run, he loves to dance, and he talks a blue streak. We watch *Singing in the Rain*, and I buy him an umbrella with rainbow stripes. He spins it on its tip on the kitchen floor, runs around it, and sings, It's raining and I'm a happy boy!

I am three and I walk behind my father as he limes the white base lines before Little League games. He has done this since before I was born, he tells me. I like drawing the lines, but balls don't interest me much, not that I could play in this league even if I wanted to. My brothers, who are born much later, play baseball every night in summer. In the winter, my father coaches basketball for the church league, so every Sunday afternoon, all winter long, we're at the gym, watching all three scheduled games. I spend most of my adult life avoiding sports.

I go to Joey's first T-ball game. Because it's Joey, and he's so happy, and they're all so cute, I go to every game. Then he's in Little League. He is attentive to everything my son teaches him, everything his coach says. He practices throwing, catching, sliding in the front yard. And he runs. Like a deer, or, as they say at Little League, he has wheels.

I love to watch him move from base to base, stealing his way home. I'm fascinated by how the boys play together, work as a team, support each other. How have I not seen this before?

I'm always asking my son, What just happened? Why is that an out? Why isn't that a home run? Baseball is full of technicalities. I discover that pitchers are not just good at throwing the ball, but at faking out the batter, setting them up for one kind of pitch then throwing another. Pitchers as Tricksters. This is a new thought for me. When Joey plays catcher, I begin to understand the communication between catcher and pitcher, how they control the game.

Joe's whole body is focused. He is lit with happiness. Through him, I learn to love baseball. We are all watching—parents and grandparents, aunts, uncles, siblings—all of us cheering plays, as if the Red Sox have just won the World Series.

Stigma

There will never be a time when it doesn't matter. It will always be there, no one will ever forget. Everyone else will be allowed to have moods, behave badly, act crazy, even. But I will not. Anything I do is a symptom, and it will always be that way. Even people I love will question, scrutinize any behavior—if I cry or laugh, or show anger or fear, if I am excited or enthusiastic, if I am sad or disgusted or disappointed; if I stay up all night or work in my PJs at noon, there will always be the question: is she crazy again?

Even if someone else is volatile, unstable, irritable, agitated. Maybe they say God talks to them. Maybe they believe in conspiracies, or that the earth is flat. They can rant, they can raise their voices, they can slam the doors of the kitchen cabinets, their laughter can fill the restaurant, they can throw a punch in a bar. They have not been diagnosed, so they do not have a mental illness, they are not crazy.

Anyone could say anything about me, and they would be right. It would be my word against theirs. And my word can't be trusted because you never know. You never know, because remember that time? That was before I was on meds, before I went to therapy for ten years. I'm not that way anymore. I can see it in their faces. They are not convinced. I could be off my meds. I have a mental illness. I am crazy forever.

What It Is For

But *what is it for?* she asks me as we drive through the forest of tiny trees. They are no more than four feet tall, these high desert trees. They are not babies, they are full grown, like the scrub pines on Cape Cod. I am lost in this nation of trees, on this road somewhere near Taos, New Mexico. I am used to the maples of the Northeast, I walk in their shade. So this is what they call a forest here. I know that's not really true—I've seen the tall pines that grow up at Los Alamos, on the mountain road I drive from Albuquerque to Santa Fe, the road I prefer because they are there. But it pleases me to be amongst this forest of tiny trees; their difference charms me. Any time I travel, I'm afraid I'll get there and it will be unfamiliar, alien, but when I step off the plane I realize, oh, yes, this is the earth, and take a trusting breath.

She is talking again, and I switch my attention from the Land outside the car to her words. But *what is it for?* she asks again. I don't understand the question. I think maybe I'm not paying close enough attention, distracted as I am by the trees. But it is the trees she is talking about. You know, she says, gesturing with her right hand as she steers with her left. All this. All this, she says, *what is it for?*

What do you mean *what is it for?*

You know, is it for farming, or dairy, or ranching . . . you know, *what is it for?*

What is it for? It's for itself, I say. She shakes her head in frustration.

This conversation has become emblematic—those moments of cultural dissonance in so many conversations, when I realize the underpinnings are different, that what I think we are talking about is not it at all.

When I was in my twenties, my then husband's aunt was concerned at what she considered my "atheism." I never said I was an atheist. It's not a word I would use, based on a negative, a lack of something, rather than on a positive presence that I felt but couldn't express. How can you not believe in God? she asked. How do you know what is good or evil? What will you teach your children?

I remember the question being so much bigger than I, at that time in my life, could answer in this short conversation over the kitchen table. I didn't know how to talk about the sacred. I felt instead an abyss, an absence of words, one that led me to become a poet. I could only tell her that I couldn't believe in that personal God, that old man in the sky. There were so many assumptions that we didn't share. I didn't yet know our Abenaki word, Ktsi Niwaskw—that sacred mysterious matrix of being, often translated as "Great Spirit."

What is it for? The language that inhabits her, that inhibits her, says that these trees, this forest, are objects. What I see as beings, as a nation of trees, she sees as, not exactly nonliving, because she would admit that trees are alive, in a limited way, but they have no sovereignty, no personhood. They exist only in relation to human needs. Which means they are expendable. This place should be "for" something that humans need. Otherwise, what?

I could say that they are "for" making oxygen, that they might hold some medicine that we don't even know about, that they hold together the soil in this arid place and provide food, make a home for a vast population of birds, insects, reptiles, mammals, invertebrates. But that is not what they are "for." These are gifts they give freely. Our proper response is gratitude.

What is it for? She turns on the radio. I look out the window. The Land extends in all its beauty, in all its mystery. This Forest, this Nation.

Happy

Two different people tell me, I can tell you're a happy person.

I hesitate. I don't know how to answer. Thank you, I say.

I think, if you only knew.

I think, but I'm happy now.

I think, am I getting manic?

Are you happy? he asks me. Every time he sees me at a birthday or holiday, my ex-husband asks me this. Are you happy?

Yes, I tell him. Yes, I'm happy. I don't tell him, my life is full, I have beautiful women friends, I am writing every day, I have birds at the window feeders, cyclamen on my kitchen table. There is a finished gourd on top of my printer that I made for my sister, the bathroom is clean. Last night I made a chicken stew. The quilts I am making for my grandsons will be done for Chanukah. I am eating fewer worms lately.

I still have days, one or two a week, when I don't get out of my PJs, and sometimes I sleep all day. Even with meds, I still cycle—this is my life. But it is never three weeks of sleeping, never a week of down days. I have a steadier life—less intense joy, less euphoria, but more a state of general happiness or enthusiasm. Sometimes I still talk a blue-streak, but I don't rage at people. And no one's moving in slo-mo.

Right now, my living room is piled with books and papers, the ironing board is covered with quilt fabric. There's a large bag of gourds in a corner waiting to be worked on, two tool boxes behind the chair. The kitchen table is cluttered with mail, books, Ikebana bowls, but the dishes are done and there's food in the fridge. I don't have a writing room/studio/office/guest room, but I have a huge desk that I keep saying is too big, but that I can't seem to get rid of. I can clean this small space without getting too overwhelmed.

I pay attention now to what triggers a swing. In high school, the nuns told us we had to avoid "occasions of sin." I'd thought I'd left all that behind. But now I find myself avoiding "occasions of mania"—evening parties, staying up all night, department stores. I avoid confrontations. I try not to take the bait.

I have rules about buying online—put everything into a cart, look at it in a week, and if I don't need it, press the delete button. This doesn't always work. If I buy one thing at a time, or secondhand, I can fool myself into buying quite a lot of stuff before I catch myself.

There is never a day when I don't have to check my mood meter, be aware of the emotional weather vane. But it has become easier, more automatic, less vigilant. I used to worry about taking meds. Now I think, What if these meds stop working?

Alnôbawôgan

We learn another word ending. Wôgan. The "ô" sounds like the French "on"-nasal, from the back of the throat. It indicates a process, a continuing. It is an ending we use with many words. It is the world in the constant process of becoming.

Awikhigan, a book. Awikhigawôgan, becoming a book. There is the writing of the book—that is the obvious meaning. The book continually becoming, as it goes out into the world, as it is read, as it becomes and becomes again for each reader, that is wôgan.

Alnôba, human being. Alnôbawôgan, becoming human. It is our word for birth. Alnôbawôgan. It also means human nature—the continual process of becoming human that we are all part of.

Alnôbawôgan. Becoming Human. It is a word of inclusion. It is the opposite of stigma. It tells me I am not so different after all. Alnôbawôgan. A word big enough to hold all of us.

it is a slow
process
becoming human
this pulling
back
this trimming
of nails
she will
roar
softly use
words
instead of
paws
she will keep
her lumbering ways
eat salmon
and blueberries
whenever
she can get them
sleep
when she pleases
wail
sometimes
sing

Acknowledgments

When I was diagnosed with rapid-cycling bipolar disorder, I needed a road map, and there wasn't one. I have written the book I wish had been there for me. All I knew at the time about bipolar/manic-depressive illness was that it had to do with mood swings and that it was one of the two "big" mental illnesses. I owe thanks to so many people who supported me through the process of learning and healing, and the writing of this book. To anyone I may have unintentionally left out, please accept my apology and gratitude.

To Lisa Brooks, my first reader, and advisor through the many stages of writing, for long conversations about storytelling and language, about wôgan, bagw, and tekw—they anchored me in place, and provided a strong framework for understanding. (For a more detailed discussion of these concepts, see her book, *The Common Pot*.) And for the great gift of your friendship, Ktsi wliwni. To Joseph Laurent and Pial Pôl Wzokhilain for their work on language, Ktsi wliwni.

To Siobhan Senier, for careful reading and listening to so many versions, for constant encouragement and support through the difficult time after diagnosis, and in so many other ways, Ktsi wliwni.

To Pam Shea, for listening to countless drafts and revisions, for your enthusiasm, belief, and encouragement, for reciting Yeats poems to me on road trips to New Hampshire, and the great gift of your friendship; to Rowena Winik for welcoming me to a community, for quietly and steadfastly believing in me, and for your courage in writing your own story, many thanks; to Diane Hebert for believing in the magic of words, thank you always; to Russell Varney for bringing me back into the world, for dinners and music and late-night conversations, thank you.

To Carol Bachofner for careful reading and feedback, Ktsi wliwni; to Cynthia Turover and Grace Lerman, for dinners of encouragement and celebration, and for lending me your home as a writing refuge; to Denise LeGault for writing time by the lake and sea, thank you; to Raven Sadhaka Seltzer, Helen Witherspoon, and Sharon Horne from the Boston Memoir Group, thank you; to Bill Siegel, for help with editing and proofreading, and for encouragement, thank you; to Sandra Conant for patience, laughter, and support; to Maura Albert and Linda Blair for listening; to Rachel Savageau for generous, honest feedback and support; to Deborah Miranda for encouraging me from the beginning, for a beautiful place to write on Cuttyhunk, for your example and friendship, Ktsi wliwni; to Margo Solod for an emphatic validation when I needed it, many thanks; to John Stanizzi for enthusiastic support and feedback, thank you; to Tony King, for support at difficult times, thank you.

I would not have been able to write this book without a network of doctors and therapists—good ones are hard to find, and I'm grateful. Thanks to Dr. Stephen Ellen, for a correct diagnosis, which I fought tooth and nail; to Dr. Michael Bohnert for guiding me through the first years of meds; to Julie Marsden, my first talk-doc, for compassion and guidance; to Karen Giuliani, who has led me through the hard work of healing and learning to cope with BP/MDI as a chronic illness, for compassion, humor, and insight, and for believing in the importance of this book, many thanks.

To everyone at University of Nebraska Press, to my editor, Matt Bokovoy, to Heather Stauffer, Ann Baker, and all the production, design, and marketing team for making this book a reality, many thanks.

It's not easy to have a family member with a major mental illness. I want to thank my extended family, for help moving and for storing my stuff until I had a place of my own, for the gift of a car when mine died, for having my piano tuned, and for willingness to listen.

To my sister, Denise Savageau, for never giving up on me, for your generosity, and for reminding me that we are strong women from a line of strong women. Thank you from my heart.

To my daughter-in-law, Marci, for inviting me into your home, for your commitment to the process of managing the illness and the family's part in that, for encouragement and feedback, thank you.

To my grandsons, Joe and Adam. The truth you spoke as little ones woke me up to my illness and gave me the determination to get well. For all you have taught me, for baseball and video games, for Ghibli afternoons, for Friday cooking and lighting candles, for the joy of being your Memere and watching you grow into good young men, you are always in my heart. Thank you.

To my son, Chris, who was there from the beginning, through good and bad, for your gifts of patience, understanding, and forgiveness, for calling it like it is, for being there through tears and rage and laughter, for saying "it goes with the territory." For giving me courage. For insightful feedback on every chapter, every story, for long conversations, for cribbage and movies and great meals. For becoming the good man you are, I am forever proud and grateful. I couldn't have done any of it without you.

SOURCE ACKNOWLEDGMENTS

Earlier versions of the poem excerpts appeared as "Crazy Woods" in *Yellow Medicine Review*, Fall 2012.

"Wet Ashes" and "Tarot": previously published in *Hinchas de Poesia* 15 (April 2015).

"When You Can't Keep a Job": previously published in *Pentimento* 5 (Summer 2015).

"Cribbage," "At the Welfare Office," and "Islands of Sanity: Poetry": previously published in *Yellow Medicine Review*, Fall 2017.

"Wretched," "Stories and Storms," "Poetry for Breakfast," and "The Death Turnpike": previously published in *Dawnland Voices 2.0* 6 (May 2018).

"The GreenQuilt": previously published in *3 Nations Anthology*, edited by Valerie Lawson (Resolute Bear Press, 2017).

An earlier version of "What It Is For" was previously published in *3 Nations Anthology*, edited by Valerie Lawson (Resolute Bear Press, 2017).

Conversations about language with Lisa Brooks were invaluable in the writing of this book and to the healing process. All mistakes are mine. For a more detailed discussion of awikhigawôgan and alnôbawôgan, see her book *The Common Pot* (University of Minnesota Press, 2008).

OTHER ACKNOWLEDGMENTS

Bly, Robert. Lines from "In This Clay Jug." In Bly, *Kabir: Ecstatic Poems*, copyright © 2004 by Robert Bly. Reprinted by permission of Beacon Press, Boston.

Brown, W. A. Seymour. Lyrics from "Oh You Beautiful Doll." 1911.

Eliot, T. S. "Preludes." In *Prufrock and Other Observations*. 1917.

Kenyon, Jane. Excerpt from "Happiness." In Kenyon, *Collected Poems*. Copyright 2005 by The Estate of Jane Kenyon. Reprinted with the permission of The Permissions Company, LLC, on behalf of Graywolf Press, www.graywolfpress.org.

Longfellow, Henry Wadsworth. "There was a little girl."

McCree, Junie. Lyrics from "Put Your Arms around Me Honey." 1910.

Poe, Edgar Allan. "The Raven," "Annabel Lee," and "The Tell-Tale Heart."

van Gogh, Vincent. "La tristesse durera toujours." Spoken on his deathbed, reported by Theo van Gogh in a letter to Elizabeth van Gogh, Paris, August 5, 1890.

Rights Remembered: A Salish Grandmother Speaks on American Indian History and the Future
By Pauline R. Hillaire
Edited by Gregory P. Fields

Essie's Story: The Life and Legacy of a Shoshone Teacher
By Esther Burnett Horne
and Sally McBeth

Song of Rita Joe: Autobiography of a Mi'kmaq Poet
By Rita Joe

Viet Cong at Wounded Knee: The Trail of a Blackfeet Activist
By Woody Kipp

Catch Colt
By Sidner J. Larson

Alanis Obomsawin: The Vision of a Native Filmmaker
By Randolph Lewis

Alex Posey: Creek Poet, Journalist, and Humorist
By Daniel F. Littlefield Jr.

The Turtle's Beating Heart: One Family's Story of Lenape Survival
By Denise Low

First to Fight
By Henry Mihesuah
Edited by Devon Abbott Mihesuah

Mourning Dove: A Salishan Autobiography
Edited by Jay Miller

I'll Go and Do More: Annie Dodge Wauneka, Navajo Leader and Activist
By Carolyn Niethammer

Tales of the Old Indian Territory and Essays on the Indian Condition
By John Milton Oskison
Edited by Lionel Larré

Elias Cornelius Boudinot: A Life on the Cherokee Border
By James W. Parins

John Rollin Ridge: His Life and Works
By James W. Parins

Singing an Indian Song: A Biography of D'Arcy McNickle
By Dorothy R. Parker

Crashing Thunder: The Autobiography of an American Indian
Edited by Paul Radin

Turtle Lung Woman's Granddaughter
By Delphine Red Shirt
and Lone Woman

Telling a Good One: The Process of a Native American Collaborative Biography
By Theodore Rios and
Kathleen Mullen Sands

Out of the Crazywoods
By Cheryl Savageau

William W. Warren: The Life, Letters,
and Times of an Ojibwe Leader
By Theresa M. Schenck

Sacred Feathers: The Reverend
Peter Jones (Kahkewaquonaby)
and the Mississauga Indians
By Donald B. Smith

Grandmother's Grandchild:
My Crow Indian Life
By Alma Hogan Snell
Edited by Becky Matthews
Foreword by Peter Nabokov

No One Ever Asked Me: The World War
II Memoirs of an Omaha Indian Soldier
By Hollis D. Stabler
Edited by Victoria Smith

Blue Jacket: Warrior of the Shawnees
By John Sugden

Muscogee Daughter: My Sojourn
to the Miss America Pageant
By Susan Supernaw
Foreword by Geary Hobson

I Tell You Now: Autobiographical
Essays by Native American Writers
Edited by Brian Swann
and Arnold Krupat

Postindian Conversations
By Gerald Vizenor and A. Robert Lee

Chainbreaker: The Revolutionary War
Memoirs of Governor Blacksnake
As told to Benjamin Williams
Edited by Thomas S. Abler

Standing in the Light:
A Lakota Way of Seeing
By Severt Young Bear
and R. D. Theisz

Sarah Winnemucca
By Sally Zanjani

To order or obtain more information on these or other University
of Nebraska Press titles, visit nebraskapress.unl.edu.

OTHER WORKS BY CHERYL SAVAGEAU

POETRY

Mother/Land
Dirt Road Home
Home Country

CHILDREN'S PICTURE BOOK

Muskrat Will Be Swimming